100 *Years* of the
U.S. OPEN

100 Years of the U.S. OPEN

John Delery and Greg Garber

FRIEDMAN/FAIRFAX
PUBLISHERS

A FRIEDMAN/FAIRFAX BOOK

Library of Congress Cataloging-in-Publication Data

Delery, John, date
    100 years of the U.S. Open / John Delery and Greg Garber.
        p.   cm.
    Rev. ed. of: Golf, 100 years of the U.S. Open. ©1993.
    Includes index.
    ISBN 1-56799-154-8
    1. United States Open Golf Championship Tournament—
History.   I. Garber, Angus G. II. Delery, John, date Golf, 100
years of the US Open.   III. Title.   IV. Title: One hundred years of
the US Open.
    GV970.D45   1995
    796.352'66—dc20
                                          94-29031
                                                CIP

Editor: Nathaniel Marunas
Art Director: Jeff Batzli
Designer: Charles Donahue
Photography Editors: Colleen Branigan and Emilya Naymark

Originally published as *Golf: 100 Years of the U.S. Open*

Additional photo credits: p.1 © Gary Newkirk/Allsport; pp. 2-3 © Richard Saker/Allsport; pp. 6–7 (Background) Culver Pictures; p. 6 © Lee Wardle; pp. 12–13 (Background) AP/Wide World Photos; p. 12 © Lee Wardle

Typeset by Classic Type, Inc.
Printed in China by Leefung-Asco Printers Ltd.

For bulk purchases and special sales, please contact:
Friedman/Fairfax Publishers
Attention: Sales Department
15 West 26th Street
New York, NY 10010
212/685-6610   FAX 212/685-1307

CONTENTS

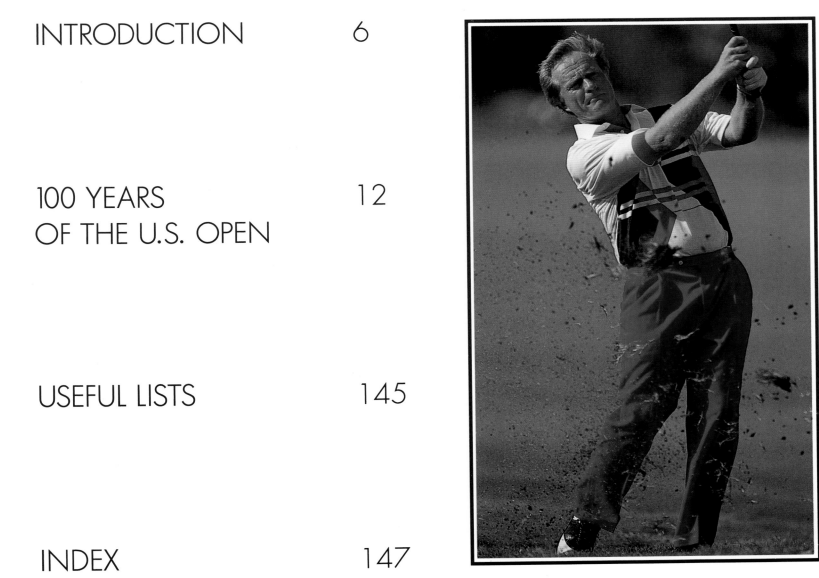

© Lee Wardle

INTRODUCTION

Lee Trevino, a championship golfer and a truth teller, doffs his cap to an adoring gallery. Trevino knows what it takes to win the U.S. Open: hard work and a straight drive off the tee.

Allsport

WHEREVER KEN VENTURI GOES, the shadow of the 1964 Open follows. "I still meet people who remember the score I shot, the year I won, and how I won," he says.

The recollections of those people should not astonish Venturi, since winning the U.S. Open is the equivalent of winning the World Series or the Super Bowl; victory alters lives, impressions, and judgments because today the entire world can witness the event and continually replay the indelible shot that usually defines an Open tournament.

"If [the Open] were the Tucson Open or the Los Angeles Open," says Lee Trevino, who won memorable U.S. Opens in 1968 and 1971, "it wouldn't be a big deal. If you lost, you'd travel to the next tournament and start over again.

"But the national championship comes around once a year. If you win that golf tournament, people realize you're an outstanding golfer."

The Open annually tightens the rack on masochists who challenge its authority. Of course, whoever overcomes this ordeal walks away with what loud, expansive game show hosts refer to as "fabulous prizes"—in this case a silver trophy and heaps of cash.

Losing the Open, however, numbs like Novocain.

Sam Snead officially won eighty-one professional golf tournaments—more than any other man—but none of them was the U.S. Open. Failing to win the Open is the one noticeable flaw in his career.

Since golf is as much about history and tradition as recreation, finishing anywhere other than first in the Open can downright torment the great golfers. "Every great golfer needs to win an Open to validate his career," Venturi says.

Until Curtis Strange won the 1988 Open championship at The Country Club in Brookline, Massachusetts, there was a divot the size of Texas on his résumé. Winning the Open automatically, though often temporarily, elevates the champion to the same level as Bobby Jones, Gene Sarazen, Ben Hogan, Arnold Palmer, Jack Nicklaus, and Tom Watson—all golfing geniuses. "I'd rather win the Open more than any other tournament," says Strange, who enjoyed the feeling so much that he won another in 1989, becoming the first golfer in thirty-eight years to successfully defend the title. (Hogan won consecutive Opens in 1950 and 1951.)

The Open champion earns more than just money; widespread recognition is commensurate with this victory. Suddenly the winner must autograph more than the bottom of his scorecard. "Usually that's great," says Strange, who craves victories more than renown, "but sometimes it's a pain in the neck."

Strange and others tolerate the pitfalls of fame because the rewards of winning an Open title offset the numerous attendant inconveniences. In addition, all the autograph requests and all the invitations to appear at exhibition matches nationwide are insignificant beside the mountain of pressure the golfer must scale to become the victor.

Gagging, after all, is the leading cause of "death" in the Open. Both throats and swings constrict more and more tightly as any golfer comes close to grasping the Holy Grail of golf. "If you have sacrificed, worked and worked as hard as you can, then the pressure's not as bad," says Trevino. "But if you're leading the Open on the last days and you haven't been putting in your practice hours, if you're wondering how the hell you got there, then you're going to feel it."

The toughest Open courses—Baltusrol Golf Club in Springfield, New Jersey; Pebble Beach Golf Links in Pebble Beach, California; Oakmont Country Club in Oakmont, Pennsylvania—comprise acres of pure hell, making matters even worse. The golf balls of prospective Open winners often vanish in the impermeable rough that the United States Golf Association (USGA) gleefully cultivates along narrow Open fairways and in front of asphalt Open greens in an attempt to weed out the good golfers from the truly special golfers. "You can win the Open putting poorly," Trevino contends, "but you can't win it driving poorly. You can win the Open with 'The Yips,' but if you're not accurate off the tee—forget it."

At the Open level, all the difficulties of an unmasterable, exasperating game converge. Instead of making approach shots, you are chopping recovery shots from grass thicker than the Beijing telephone book and begging the pitiless golf gods to be merciful. Shaved greens smoother than Italian marble cause people who never even three-putt to four-putt on some of the fastest greens in tournament golf. "The U.S. Open throws so much at you over seventy-two holes, so you have to be tough to win," Strange says. "I try to clear my mind each round...resolve to going to war [from Thursday to Sunday]."

Open courses do not require goofy railroad ties or grassy humps the size of the Alps to terrify competitors. Fairways thinner than Jane Fonda and putting surfaces harder to read than federal income tax forms, not gimmicks, mark an Open battleground. "The USGA," Trevino says, "is living proof that you don't need any of that tricky stuff to produce a terrifying course. The USGA takes those seventy-, eighty-year-old courses, narrows the fairways, lets the rough grow, hardens the greens, turns you loose and makes a fool out of you."

The Open often humiliates golfers lucky to have landed in the field of 156 contenders, and occasionally inspires others—Ben Hogan for one. Hogan won four Opens in all, a record he shares with Willie Anderson, Jones, and Nicklaus. Winning the Open was Hogan's compulsion. He constantly drove both himself and practice golf balls in order to be the best, though success eluded him for some time. Hogan was thirty-six years old before he finally won the Open in 1948.

He had to wait until 1950 to try again, because he nearly lost his life in a car accident. Hogan shot 69 in overtime at Merion that year and won a playoff against Lloyd Mangrum and George Fazio. He won his third Open in 1951 and his fourth in 1953.

Predictable champions such as Hogan generally reach the top of the leaderboard at the Open and regularly leave the Open course of the year toting their clubs, the trophy, and the enviable paycheck.

Surprise endings, though, occasionally punctuate the Open with an enormous question mark. Some observers still wonder, for instance, how someone like Andy North could win two Opens in eight years.

The Open remains interesting because sometimes the grinders of golf—methodical men who survey each shot interminably while sniffing the wind and tossing tufts of grass into air currents indiscernible to spectators—join the elite club of Open winners.

Golf history treats certain Open champions with more reverence than others, but no amount of disdain can erase the name of any Open champion from the trophy or the golf pantheon. "There's no such thing as a former Open champion," Ken Venturi says. "They're all Open champions. Period."

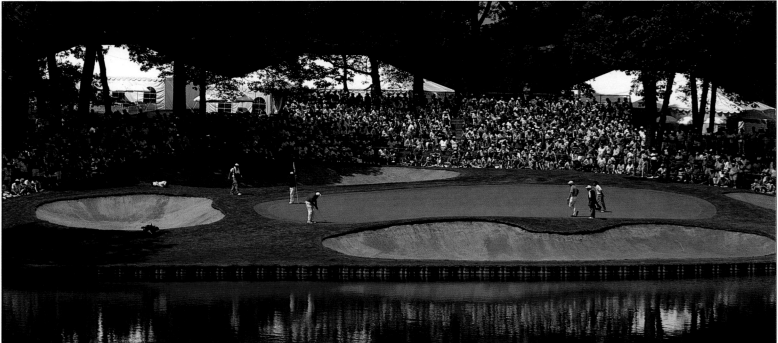

© Lee Wardle

U.S. Open courses are something special; they all have tradition and a ruthlessly rugged layout designed to test a golfer's body and soul. Medinah Country Club (OPPOSITE PAGE) *in Chicago, seen here from the seventeenth hole, played host to the Open in 1990. Strange things happen when a man is tested in the crucible of the U.S. Open. Andy North* (LEFT), *a golfer who previously had only a single victory to his credit, won the Open in 1978 and again in 1985.*

100 YEARS
OF THE U.S. OPEN

Horace Rawlins, an Englishman who had caddied on the Isle of Wight, was the first man to win the U.S. Open. He took home $150 and a gold medal.

PGA World Golf Hall of Fame

1 8 9 5

NEWPORT GOLF CLUB
NEWPORT · RHODE ISLAND

In the beginning, the best American golfers were European men with U.S. roots thinner than dental floss. Americans were too busy falling in love with baseball—another sport with an elusive white ball—to immediately embrace golf, an equally cruel and addictive game.

Today, the world enters, covers, and watches the U.S. Open, but the first championship in 1895 did not attract much attention or many golfers. Horace Rawlins of England, an assistant at the host course, beat nine British professionals, including his boss, Willie Davis, and one Canadian amateur at the Newport Golf Club, then nine holes of alternately swampy and craggy topography. He won $150 and a gold medal.

The purse is more than 1,800 times that amount these days, but Open champions of the present usually have the same attitude as the Open pioneers did: golfing immortality and the trophy are more important than the paycheck.

Willie Dunn, Jr., Willie Campbell, and Jim Foulis, good golfers all, were the favorites in the inaugural Open, a one-day walking tour of manorly Rhode Island. The odds of Rawlins winning were shorter than the course, which was merely 2,755 yards long, but he did not figure to intimidate or defeat the field at the age of twenty.

Dunn, Campbell, and Foulis each shot 89 and led at the end of eighteen holes. Scores like that now would leave contestants closer to last place than first, and players who made such scores would not survive the cut. It is important to remember, of course, that this was prior to the age of square grooves and men strong enough to launch "hot balls" into contiguous orbit with Pluto. Golfers then were essentially belting stones with crooked hickory sticks. Rawlins shot 45 and 46 for a total of 91 over the first eighteen holes. Then, with birdies on the first and eighth holes, he shot 41 on the third nine to move into second place, one stroke behind Campbell.

Campbell, the professional at The Country Club, lost his golf ball, aim, composure, and lead at the third hole of the final round, a par-three, merely 165 yards long. His second tee ball wound up lodging against the base of a stone wall. He left the hole scratching nine on his scorecard, shot 48 on the championship nine, and fell from first to fourth at 179.

Rawlins reproduced his 41 on the third nine and outshot Dunn by two strokes, 173 to 175, at the first Open conducted by the new USGA. Foulis and A.W. Smith, the Canadian amateur, placed third at 176.

The first Open, like the initial Super Bowl, begat nothing more than a champion. Open mania did not materialize instantly.

1 8 9 6

**SHINNECOCK HILLS GOLF CLUB
SOUTHAMPTON · NEW YORK**

The Open field in 1896 was three times the size it had been in 1895, but the tournament did not outgrow its standing as an inferior sideshow to the U.S. Amateur. In those days, professional golfers were more unpopular at country clubs than increases in dues and membership fees. In the eyes of the golfing aristocracy, amateurs were gentlemen and pros were crude rogues. In all, there were thirty-five entrants and twenty-eight finishers in the second Open, Jim Foulis' Open. Foulis, third the previous year, beat both Horace Rawlins, the first Open champion, and Shinnecock Hills, a troublesome course.

Shinnecock Hills, then just 4,423 yards long, is not an authentic links layout because it is too far inland and does not exactly touch water. It is, however, a good facsimile. It is open, and the few trees on the course often become irrelevant during rounds. Shinnecock Hills is also a scrubby course, a heathland minefield.

The Indian grass that lines much of the fairways generally stands one foot or taller. Beyond the Indian grass lurk the fragrant, but treacherous, beach plum and bayberry bushes—sinister shrubbery indeed. The thorny beach plum and bayberry bushes can prick the fingers, legs, and psyche of the golfer unfortunate and inaccurate enough to land in them. The one symbolic similarity between Shinnecock Hills and the links of Scotland and England is the wind, which whips off the Atlantic

Third the previous year, Jim Foulis, a club professional from Chicago, won the second U.S. Open, in 1896.

Ocean and Peconic Bay and threatens to launch golfers and their golf balls into orbit.

All the botanical booby traps and the blustery conditions did not prevent Foulis from upstaging both Rawlins and Shinnecock Hills. He shot 152 over thirty-six holes—74 on the second eighteen, the scoring record for one round until 1903.

Rawlins came close to defending his title: he finished second, only three shots behind Foulis. While he did not win another Open, Rawlins was already ensured a place at the top of an illustrious list of Open victors.

1 8 9 7

CHICAGO GOLF CLUB
WHEATON · ILLINOIS

Jim Foulis' home course advantage did not help him against Englishman Joe Lloyd, the last champion over thirty-six holes. (The Open was soon lengthened to seventy-two holes.) Lloyd won the final subordinate Open—held between the semifinals and finals of the Amateur—with scores of 83 and 79 at the Chi-

Hobbs Golf Collection

cago Golf Club. His total of 162 beat thirty-four competitors, among them the runner-up, young Willie Anderson of Scotland, who later won four Open titles in five years beginning in 1901. Foulis, the previous titlist, wound up sharing third place.

The course of American golf history began to change after the 1897 Open. In order to inject some prestige into the event and slowly shape it into the U.S. equivalent of the majestic British Open, the USGA decided to separate its Open from the Amateur and extend the tournament to seventy-two holes, beginning in 1898. The idea was to create an unmistakably grand golf tournament to challenge that of the British, whose Royal and Ancient Golf Club vainly referred to its top tournament as "The Open Championship," as if there were no other.

Suddenly, Americans were intent on adopting golf, a game born sometime in the 1400s at St. Andrews Golf Club in Scotland, one of the auldest courses on Earth.

1 8 9 8

MYOPIA HUNT CLUB
SOUTH HAMILTON · MASSACHUSETTS

Actually, the new format of the tournament did not instantly attract the finest foreign golfers to American turf—though the field grew to forty-nine men—or greatly improve the level of play. The location, however, was perfect. What better site to launch a revolution against the British Empire than Massachusetts, the seat of American secessionists 122 years earlier?

Scotsman Fred Herd, the professional at Washington Park in Chicago, won the title by averaging 82 over four rounds, or

OPPOSITE PAGE: *This motley crew includes some of the best golfers of the day, Horace Rawlins and Alex Smith among them.* RIGHT: *Typical of the professionals of his day, Fred Herd, winner of the 1898 Open, drank heavily and was liberal in his use of colorful language.*

Hobbs Golf Collection

eight tours of Myopia Hunt Club, which consisted of nine oppressive holes. Herd was six shots behind at the end of the first round and broke 84 only once, but he won by seven strokes, defeating Alex Smith of Scotland 328 to 335. The USGA, fearful Herd would pawn the Open trophy to pay for a victory celebration at some saloon, required him to leave collateral for it.

This historical note follows that hysterical note: Willie Anderson, representing Baltusrol Golf Club, wound up third, one notch below his close friend Willie Smith and one place lower than his finish in the 1897 Open. It is no wonder that Anderson spent the last portion of the century quietly sharpening his game, which would peak in the early 1900s.

1 8 9 9

BALTIMORE COUNTRY CLUB
BALTIMORE · MARYLAND

In 1899 there were two U.S. Opens: one pitting Willie Smith against history and another among Smith and the remaining eighty men in the field. The other entrants spent almost the entire tournament searching for Smith at the Baltimore Country Club. He rudely hid from the pack during most of the fifth Open.

In the end there were 11 strokes between Smith and the runners-up, Val Fitzjohn, George Low, and W. H. Way. Strangely, the talent gap between Smith and the field was not supposed to be as wide as the margin of victory, still the largest in Open history, would indicate. Smith, part of a clan of able golfers from Carnoustie, Scotland, broke 80 in all but one round. He shot 77 in the first round, 82 in the second, and 79 in the third. He finished the Open the way he began it, with another 77.

The purse rose to $650 that year, but Smith's record victory was worth $150 just the same. Little as it was, however, his take from the tournament probably lasted longer than his fame. Willie Smith apparently spent himself over those two days; he never regained the Open title, though he came close twice. Smith lost to his brother, Alex, at the Onwentsia Club in 1906 and to Fred McLeod in a playoff at the Myopia Hunt Club in 1908.

Hobbs Golf Collection

Willie Smith's winning margin of 11 strokes is the largest in Open history; curiously enough, Smith subsequently never lived up to this record achievement.

1 9 0 0

CHICAGO GOLF CLUB
WHEATON · ILLINOIS

The first five U.S. Opens were a false start. The tournament truly began in 1900 when Harry Vardon, one of the original golfing gods, entered and won the event, validating the Open with the equivalent of a papal blessing. The chance to promote his line of Spalding golf balls—the Vardon Flyer—drew him to the Chicago Golf Club more than the opportunity to mount the U.S. Open trophy beside his three British Open keepsakes. (As it turned out, Wheaton was just another stop on his victory tour of North America: in addition to the Open title, he won more than fifty exhibition matches from Canada to Florida during that year.)

His strength, talent, and graceful swing, however, were even more impressive than his victory total. His promotional matches were invaluable golf lessons because they taught Americans how to follow and enjoy the game. Jerry Travers, who became one of the top amateur golfers in the United States, spoke admiringly about Harry Vardon: "If you run across the man who is making the game so easy a child could play it, whose form is the last word in poetry and who from 180 to 220 yards is putting a full shot closer to the hole than most others can put a mashie, your quest for Vardon will be over."

In the first Open of the twentieth century, Vardon and J. H. Taylor, champion of the British Open three times (including 1900), were the favorites and the best golfers in an excellent field. Not surprisingly, the 1900 U.S. Open was a thrilling duel between Vardon and Taylor.

Taylor did not seem too confident at the outset because he disliked the greens—in fact, he likened them to a boy's hair brushed in the wrong direction. (Greenskeepers today meticulously groom each individual blade of grass, or so it seems, but years ago, before modern methods of agronomy, putting surfaces were usually bumpier than backwoods roads.) At any rate, Taylor sank enough putts to lead at the end of the first round. He shot 76, three fewer strokes than Vardon, who did not putt well.

People began noticing the U.S. Open, still the little brother of the British Open at the time, when the great Harry Vardon won the event in 1900.

Vardon shot 78 in the afternoon and overtook Taylor at the end of round two. Uncharacteristic carelessness at the eighteenth hole cost Vardon one shot of his lead. He mishit his par putt, and then embarrassed himself by whiffing on his next stroke when the blade of his putter got tangled in the stiff grass. He added three shots to his lead in the third round, shooting 76, his lowest score of the tournament.

In the end, Vardon shot 80, Taylor 78. Vardon won 313 to 315. Vardon did more than just win the Open, though—he unofficially christened it by introducing a new level of play.

1 9 0 1

MYOPIA HUNT CLUB
SOUTH HAMILTON · MASSACHUSETTS

Although Harry Vardon, "King of Swing I," had instilled a new excitement in the Open in 1900, the tournament still did not take off like a perfectly struck drive. National interest in the event did not grow remarkably until a virtually unknown golfer crammed the winner's take into the side pocket of his tartan plaid pants every year but one from 1901 to 1905.

America noticed the Open more when Willie Anderson of Scotland began collecting titles in the same manner countless children collect baseball cards—regularly. Anderson had spent the last years of the 1890s approaching fame from the shadows, narrowly losing the 1897 Open to Joe Lloyd at the age of seventeen, then finishing third at the 1898 Open and fifth at the 1899 Open.

Although "mysterious" describes him better than "good," Anderson stands out in golf history because he won four Opens in all (the same number as Jack Nicklaus, Ben Hogan, and Bobby Jones) and three consecutively beginning in 1903. He won his first Open title at the Myopia Hunt Club in 1901, defeating his best friend, Alex Smith of Scotland, in an alternately sensational and ugly duel.

The course had grown considerably since the last time the Greatest Show on Turf came to town in 1898. Myopia was double its previous size—now eighteen holes measuring 6,130 yards. In fact, club selection did not stump the golfers so much as deciding what to complain about first: the length of the

Hobbs Golf Collection

course or its degree of difficulty. The fairways were hard and the greens were as slick as ice, causing countless putts to slide past the cup, and some to slip off the putting surface altogether.

Laurie Auchterlonie led at the end of the first round. He shot an 81, one stroke better than Alex Smith. Later, Smith's second 82 put him ahead of the field halfway through what was proving to be the tightest tournament yet. Stewart Gardner replaced Smith at the top after fifty-four holes. One shot separated Gardner and Anderson, who was in second place with an aggregate score of 250. In all, six golfers were within three shots of the leader: Anderson, Alex Smith, Auchterlonie, David Brown, Bernard Nicholls, and Willie Smith.

Anderson shot an 81 in the fourth round and sure did look like the champion. In order just to match Anderson's 331 total, Alex Smith somehow would have to manage three fours on the final three holes. The odds did not favor him, but Smith did not march off the course, enter the clubhouse, exchange swords with Anderson, and announce, "I surrender." Instead, he sank a long putt for a three on the sixteenth hole, but offset the birdie with a bogey at the seventeenth hole. In order to tie Anderson now, he definitely needed a four on the last hole.

The eighteenth hole did not look overly treacherous, measuring a measly 335 yards, but golf tests nerves more than muscles. Besides the lowest score, the Open champion usually needs the bravest putting stroke.

Smith drove perfectly, then struck an approach shot to within ten feet of the cup. He was that close to winning the Open. He misread the speed of the green, however, and mishit the birdie putt. The ball rolled toward the center of the hole, but stopped an inch or two short. He tapped it in and tied Anderson.

The two shared the lead for three days—the playoff was delayed that long because the course was reserved for club members throughout the weekend. In the end, Anderson barely won the title in overtime, shooting 85 to Smith's 86, but Anderson stood on the fringe of greatness.

Hobbs Golf Collection

OPPOSITE PAGE: *Willie Anderson* (LEFT) *and Alex Smith.* RIGHT: *Anderson became a golfing legend by winning four Opens before the age of thirty, when he died of what was officially referred to as arteriosclerosis (many claimed alcohol was his undoing).*

Hobbs Golf Collection

GARDEN CITY GOLF CLUB
GARDEN CITY · NEW YORK

Creating a sturdier, controllable, obliging golf ball has been the obsession of golf enthusiasts since the inception of the game. In the early seventeenth century, golf balls were misshapen leather pouches full of goose feathers and surprising life. These "featheries" flew tremendous distances but had a major shortcoming besides their considerable expense: they were extremely fragile.

"Gutties" were the durable successor to featheries. Gutties were golf balls handmade from gutta-percha, a gum extract from Malaysia. Gutties were smooth as billiard balls until the 1870s, when some perceptive golfers noticed that the ball flew longer and truer with nicks on its exterior.

Gutties were the first revolutionary advance in the long history of the sport because they were much cheaper than featheries, perfectly round, and practically indestructible.

In 1902 the modern, durable golf ball was born. It was made in three pieces with a rubber core around which hundreds of yards of thin rubber thread was wound. The core was then encased in gutta-percha. This design improvement added about twenty-five to fifty yards to drives and immeasurably changed the game.

Traditionalists, afraid the invention would adulterate their pristine sport, initially disregarded the sturdier, livelier ball, the creation of Coburn Haskell of Cleveland, Ohio. Professionals also snubbed the ball in the beginning, believing it too uncontrollable. What advantage is extra distance if the ball only flies farther into the woods?

Pros eventually lost their inhibitions and the scores in the 1902 Open reflected the new muscular approach to golf, a game which had previously been an exercise in precision rather than strength.

Laurie Auchterlonie won the title in 1902 by breaking 80 in every round, a first. His total of 307, the record until 1904, left him six shots ahead of amateur Walter Travis and professional Stewart Gardner. Auchterlonie shot so consistently, he shot in the forties in only two sets.

1 9 0 3

BALTUSROL GOLF CLUB
SPRINGFIELD · NEW JERSEY

In the middle of the 1890s, Willie Anderson, a vagabond golfer from North Berwick, Scotland, began going from club to club in America searching for teaching jobs and answers to a puzzling game. He carried the solution to this demonic diversion in his golf bag during the beginning of the 1900s.

Anderson, the Open champion in 1901, won his second title in 1903, this time at Baltusrol Golf Club, his workplace five years before. This title opened the victory spigot for Anderson: the 1904 and 1905 Opens were his Opens, too. Willie Anderson may have been the finest American golfer at the time, but who knew? He lived in the shadows, not the limelight, and was alternately proud, pugnacious, and silent during his career, which was not much shorter than his life.

His remoteness on any course often was the result of his desire and need to play golf in a trance. He outshot so many opponents because he outthought so many opponents. Anderson's swing was as flat as his nose, and neither his game nor his facial features were flattering or classical. He looked more like an average middleweight boxer than a special golfer. He had bulging forearms and wide, muscular shoulders, a physique more suitable for someone lugging blocks of ice door-to-door instead of a golf bag from course to course.

Golfers of Willie Anderson's time essentially wore clothes formal enough to attend church in, but not Willie Anderson. His typical attire was a tartan wool cap pulled low (to camouflage his large ears), baggy plaid trousers, a plain shirt, a cloth neckerchief (instead of a silk tie), and an old tweed jacket.

Anderson did have one thing in common with his peers: a desire to imitate Harry Vardon. Early golfers gauged their success using an unreasonable caliper: how would I measure up to Vardon?

Laurie Auchterlonie (OPPOSITE PAGE) *won the 1902 U.S. Open by breaking 80 in every round, a first. The enigmatic Willie Anderson* (RIGHT) *won the second of his four U.S. Open titles at Baltusrol Golf Club in 1903.*

While early golf historians ignored Anderson, recent observers of the game believe Anderson may have been as good as any golfer from his era, including Vardon.

Too many golfers spend most of their round in the trees, hunting for their ball, comforting the small game they have struck with yet another misdirected shot. Spectators searching for Anderson usually found him in the middle of the fairway. He may have been the most accurate golfer of his period, particularly with a mashie, the equivalent of the modern five-iron.

In the 1903 Open Anderson knew the course better than anyone in the field, and he played like someone with special knowledge until the fourth round. He shot 73 in the first round, then a record round. He was in position to challenge Willie Smith's record for widest margin of victory at the end of three rounds—he led by six shots. When he shot an 82 in the fourth round, however, Anderson lost all of his advantage. He wound up sharing first place at 307 with another Scotsman, David Brown, an erstwhile plasterer who had not won a major golf tournament in seventeen years.

The result of the playoff was more notable than the ordinary scores of the playoff: Anderson shot an 82, Brown an 84. The victory meant Anderson became the first man to win two Open titles, and put him alongside the inaugural champion, Horace Rawlins, on the roster of special golfers in U.S. Open annals.

1 9 0 4

GLEN VIEW CLUB
GOLF · ILLINOIS

Modest Willie Anderson made history in 1903 and no noise afterwards. Renown did not reroute his train of thought; he remained distant, silent, and ambitious, all of which are Ben Hogan traits. Indeed, most of the exceptional golf champions in history have had these single-minded characteristics.

Anderson drove himself as hard as he drove his golf ball whenever he had an opportunity to win a golf tournament. He thought of golf as his job, not a game to play frivolously. So, he approached the game as if he were a furious bull charging a matador: head down at stampede speed.

He had the 1904 Open in his cross hairs from the beginning of the tournament. Anderson shot 75 in the first round, but had to share the lead with Stewart Gardner. He fell back in the second and third rounds, shooting successive 78s.

Fred McKenzie led by two strokes at the end of three rounds, but retreating did not interest Anderson. He thought the only way to catch up, to overtake McKenzie and seize his reward, was to attack the Glen View Club and the field.

Anderson went for broke and struck it rich. He began the fourth round with four consecutive fours and one three. He went out in 37 and came home in 35, playing the last eight holes in two under par, unheard of golf at the time. His 72 in the final round and his total of 303 were records. In the end, Anderson beat Gil Nicholls by five shots.

Willie Anderson unexpectedly became the first man to win three Opens and the first man to successfully defend the title. Enrichment came from the accomplishment, because he won successive Opens long before the era of purses with six zeroes in the total and fat endorsement jackpots for the champion.

1 9 0 5

MYOPIA HUNT CLUB
SOUTH HAMILTON · MASSACHUSETTS

Willie Anderson arrived at Myopia as the clear favorite in 1905. After all, the slight Scotsman had won three of the four previous U.S. Opens and at age twenty-five seemed destined to dominate the event in a way no one might ever match. But Anderson stumbled to an opening round of 80, a daunting five strokes behind Alex Smith and Stewart Gardner. Confidence, however, was not something Anderson lacked. He fired a 76 in the third round and, with eighteen holes to play, trailed Smith by a single stroke.

The final day's result was almost a foregone conclusion. Smith, playing ahead of Anderson, was fairly uninspired and wound up shooting his third consecutive 80. Anderson had an adventure or two along the way (he bogeyed the twelfth and thirteenth holes), but he pulled himself together in time for the finishing hole. He struck a typically accurate drive off

Alex Smith won the 1906 U.S. Open with a blazing (by turn-of-the-century standards) 295. Here, he displays his aggressive style off the eighth tee.

Culver Pictures

the tee, played a conservative pitch to the green, and two-putted for a closing round of 77. And though Anderson's 314 looked less than elegant on his scorecard, it was good for his fourth U.S. Open title in five years, an achievement of staggering dimension.

Consider that only three other golfers would win four U.S. Opens: Bobby Jones captured four titles in a span of eight years, from 1923 to 1930; Ben Hogan triumphed four times in the six years between 1948 and 1953; and Jack Nicklaus managed the same feat over an eighteen-year period, from 1962 to 1980. But never did anyone so thoroughly embarrass his peers in an event of such importance.

That was Anderson's gift; he rose to the important occasions. Unfortunately, he never had the chance to age gracefully in the game. He did not win another U.S. Open title, and he died of arteriosclerosis four years later at the age of thirty.

1 9 0 6

ONWENTSIA CLUB
LAKE FOREST · ILLINOIS

Heading into the 1906 U.S. Open, Alex Smith wondered if he would ever beat Willie Anderson on a championship course. The painful loss of 1901 was still in his memory: Anderson had erased a five-stroke deficit in five holes and forced the first play-off in Open history. Smith's 86 had been one stroke short of Anderson's 85. Then in 1905, it happened again: Anderson fashioned a 314 over four rounds, two strokes better than Smith's 316. Smith had also been the second-place finisher to Fred Herd at the Myopia Club in 1898. And, in a twist of fate, Anderson had taken the professional's job at Onwentsia and was considered the overwhelming tournament favorite.

Smith, steady as he was congenial, led Anderson by two strokes after the first day's thirty-six holes. Inexplicably, Anderson never made the move Smith and the rest of the field anticipated. He shot a game 74 in the third round, but lost a stroke to Smith, who seemed to grow stronger as the day went on. Anderson fell apart in the fourth round, falling to a dismal 84, while Smith registered a 75 that broke new ground on several levels.

RIGHT: *Alex Ross, always the gentleman, became the seventh consecutive Scotsman to win the U.S. Open. He fired four consistent rounds in the middle 70s to triumph at the Philadelphia Cricket Club in 1907.* OPPOSITE PAGE: *In 1908, in the last of four U.S. Open staged at the Myopia Hunt Club in South Hamilton, Massachusetts, Fred McLeod emerged as the winner.*

For starters, Smith became the first man to break 300 in a U.S. Open with a searing 295. For this, he took home the $300 winner's prize. Secondly, Alex and Willie, who finished seven strokes behind, became the first brothers to capture U.S. Opens. After finishing as the runner-up to Anderson twice, Smith had distinguished himself as the champion.

1 9 0 7

PHILADELPHIA CRICKET CLUB
PHILADELPHIA · PENNSYLVANIA

By now, Scotland's mastery in the U.S. Open was pronounced. At the turn of the century, several hundred young Scots had left the village of Carnoustie for America, where they played and taught the game. Through the first six contests, Britain and Scotland had three champions each. Then, beginning with Willie Anderson in 1901, the Scots had run off six consecutive victories. In 1907, Alex Ross made it a magnificent seven.

Ross was the model of consistency on the old St. Martins course, shooting 76, 74, 76, 76 for a tidy 302. Gil Nicholls, who had been second to Willie Anderson in 1904, was second again with a 304.

1 9 0 8

MYOPIA HUNT CLUB
SOUTH HAMILTON · MASSACHUSETTS

Golf has always been an egalitarian sport. In basketball, the taller man has the best chance to succeed, just as the bigger man has the advantage in football. Golf, however, like soccer and baseball, places a premium on intelligence, pure athletic skill, and timing.

So it was that a diminutive Scotsman named Fred McLeod won the 1908 U.S. Open at the Myopia Hunt Club, the fourth and final time the event was staged there. McLeod was not especially long off the tee, but his game had a certain precision, particularly around the greens. When McLeod wound up

the four-round tournament tied with Willie Smith at 322, most observers presumed that Smith, the 1899 Open champion, would walk away from McLeod in the playoff. Instead, McLeod fired a 77 under the intense pressure of the extra round, beating Smith by a wide margin of six strokes. At 108 pounds, McLeod became the smallest U.S. Open winner in history, before or since.

Culver Pictures

George Sargent scored 290 over 72 holes in 1902, setting a scoring record that would last for seven years.

The Illustrated London News Picture Library

1 9 0 9

ENGLEWOOD GOLF CLUB
ENGLEWOOD · NEW JERSEY

It was 1909 and the spirit of adventure was in the air. Admiral Robert Peary had finally broken through on his sixth attempt to reach the North Pole on April 6. In golf, there was another movement afoot: the Americans were on the verge of their own breakthrough in the U.S. Open. For years, fourteen to be precise, golfers from across the Atlantic had won the U.S. championship. As time went on, however, Americans began to close the gap.

The first round of the 1909 Open was marked by Dave Hunter's scintillating 68, which was the first sub-70 round in Open history. Then, after two rounds, American professional Tom McNamara, who had opened with a 69, found himself leading the tournament. Alas, George Sargent, a seasoned professional from England, closed strongly and set a new aggregate record, 290, to edge McNamara by four strokes. But the gauntlet had been thrown down; the Americans were on the threshold, about to rise to this grand occasion.

1 9 1 0

PHILADELPHIA CRICKET CLUB
PHILADELPHIA · PENNSYLVANIA

The Smith brothers, Willie and Alex, had already left their mark on the U.S. Open when younger brother Macdonald left Carnoustie, Scotland, for the United States in 1910. Willie and Alex had each won the Open and now Macdonald, barely past his twentieth birthday, seemed likely to follow in the family tradition. But age, after faltering slightly, had its day at the Philadelphia Cricket Club.

Alex, now a venerable thirty-eight, had a one-stroke lead on the seventy-second hole, but inexplicably missed a three-foot putt for the championship. That mistake allowed two far younger hands back into the tournament. Young Macdonald had fired a startling 71 in the final round to force a playoff with his brother and an eighteen-year-old American named Johnny McDermott, the son of a Philadelphia mailman.

Sunday was a day of rest, so the playoff was contested on Monday, a fortuitous turn of events for Alex Smith. After a day off to steady his nerves, Alex was never challenged by the upstarts. He shot a 71, while McDermott finished with a 75 and Macdonald struggled in with a 77. It was the second Open championship for Alex, making him only the second man, after Willie Anderson, to record a double. Alex would never win another Open and, surprisingly, his younger brother Macdonald would never win one. The same could not be said for McDermott, who would soon make golfing history.

1 9 1 1

CHICAGO GOLF CLUB
WHEATON · ILLINOIS

Johnny McDermott was nineteen when he teed off in the 1911 U.S. Open outside Chicago. Like most successful athletes, however, he was older than his years; he had developed his impressive skills through painstaking practice. He dropped out of high school and took professional jobs at various New Jersey clubs. Before and after his duties in the pro shop, McDermott worked on his game, lofting shot after shot into the coming light or gathering darkness. After his second-place finish in the 1910 U.S. Open, McDermott honed his game against Philadelphia professionals. He beat them routinely.

The field at the Chicago Golf Club, however, was far deeper than McDermott was accustomed to, and the conditions were close to impossible. The June sun blazed, drying the greens and leaving them treacherous. Alex Ross, the 1907 Open winner, was the only golfer to master the course; his 74 was the best score over the first round. McDermott shot a less-than-impressive 81, but rebounded with a 72 later in the day. Through the third and fourth rounds, it became clear this was a tournament no one wanted to win. McDermott stumbled through the second day with scores of 75 and 79, while Mike Brady, another young American, and George Simpson scratched their way to identical scores of 307.

UPI/Bettmann

He wasn't big and he wasn't very old, but Johnny McDermott could work a golf ball. At the age of nineteen he bested the field at the 1911 U.S. Open. After losing in 1910 in a playoff, McDermott won this time, becoming the youngest golfer ever to win the event.

Thus, for the second time in as many years, McDermott found himself in a three-way playoff for the U.S. Open. The lesson of 1910, apparently, was not lost on him. His first two shots off the first tee flew out of bounds and he scored a six on the first hole, dropping him two behind Brady and one behind Simpson. McDermott rallied quickly, however, and left Brady and Simpson in his wake after nine holes. The final scores: McDermott 80, Brady 82, and Simpson 85.

There it was: Johnny McDermott simultaneously became the youngest player ever to win the U.S. Open and the first American-born to capture the championship. For the first time, a native golfer had shown he could not only compete with the imported players from Scotland and Britain, but beat them in the country's most meaningful tournament as well. Mike Brady's second-place finish underlined America's growing dominance in the field of professional golf.

ever, had become a factor. He shot a 35 on the front nine holes, then fashioned three birdies on the next four holes. McNamara finished with a terrific 69, good for an aggregate of 296, putting enormous pressure on McDermott. But McDermott was up to it; he shot a 71 for a winning total of 294, bettering par by two strokes, the first time such a thing had happened.

McDermott, quite full of himself, had now won back-to-back Open titles before the age of twenty-one. Strangely, he would never win another. A series of misfortunes, among them some ill-advised stock investments that ended in a shipwreck in the English Channel, robbed him of his confidence and powers of concentration. McDermott's fall from grace didn't upset many of the British and Scottish golfers, who believed the young American and some of his peers were too cocky for their own good. An epic battle between the established professionals from Britain and the rising Americans would soon take place.

1 9 1 2

THE COUNTRY CLUB OF BUFFALO
BUFFALO · NEW YORK

Public interest in the U.S. Open had heretofore been tepid. The small band of talented professionals had made the tournament an artistic success, but the masses were still in the dark. The U.S. Amateur championship was still more highly regarded and regularly drew twice as many entries. McDermott's victory in the 1911 Open helped spark interest in the championship, though. While the number of entries generally fluctuated between seventy and ninety, the 1912 Open boasted an unprecedented field of 131 golfers, 130 of them determined to prevent McDermott from repeating his victory.

The concept of "par" golf had been established the year before, but nothing prepared the keepers of the long course for the beating it was about to take. Both Mike Brady and Alex Smith stood at 147 after thirty-six holes, one shot under the par standard of 74. McDermott lurked two shots behind. After three rounds, Brady led McDermott by three shots.

In the final round McDermott started quickly and crushed the hopes of Brady, who began miserably. Tom McNamara, how-

1 9 1 3

THE COUNTRY CLUB
BROOKLINE · MASSACHUSETTS

When British stars Harry Vardon and J. H. Taylor toured America in 1900, one of their stops was the U.S. Open at the Chicago Golf Club. Vardon finished first, with a 313, and Taylor was two strokes behind in second place. While their presence lent a new credibility to the tournament, their performance merely confirmed that the golf professionals from across the Atlantic were far superior to the Americans.

Thirteen years later, much had changed. The U.S. Open still ran second to the U.S. Amateur in terms of public awareness, but it was becoming recognized as the nation's definitive professional tournament. At the same time, the successes of young American professionals like Johnny McDermott, Tom McNamara, and Mike Brady suggested that the days of foreign dominance might soon be over.

The Country Club (OPPOSITE PAGE), *in Brookline, Massachusetts, and its picturesque seventeenth hole were the scene of one of the Open's most memorable moments.*

Still, when it was learned that Vardon and countryman Ted Ray were returning to America, under the sponsorship of newspaper baron Lord Northcliffe, observers wondered if American golfers were up to the task of defending McDermott's title. Vardon was an elegant striker of the ball; Ray was a muscular force off the tee. They were immediately installed as co-favorites.

Coming into the late September tournament, Vardon and Ray were on a hot streak. They had challenged the best of the Americans in a series of exhibitions, and they had won almost every time out. As a result of the Englishmen's successes, interest in the 1913 U.S. Open swelled, as did the entries. A total of 165 golfers were in the field at the Country Club, surpassing the record of 131 set the previous year. Walter Hagen, a confident twenty-year-old golfer from Rochester, New York, was one of them. Francis Ouimet, also aged twenty, was another.

© Alex MacLean

Francis Ouimet, a mere stripling, won the U.S. Open in 1913, which resulted in a great rise in American interest in the sport.

While Hagen was a professional, Ouimet was still an amateur. He had begun caddying around Brookline at the age of eleven and developed a fondness for the game. He practiced endlessly on the Franklin Park public course and sometimes, early in the morning, he'd sneak onto the elegant Country Club layout. By the age of sixteen, Ouimet was the Boston Interscholastic champion. And though he failed in three consecutive attempts to qualify for the U.S. Amateur tournament, Ouimet, a sports shop clerk, finally broke through in 1913. He lost to three-time winner Jerry Travers in the second round, but it was a tight match and Ouimet drew some confidence from it.

The Scots went out quickly at Brookline, with Macdonald Smith and Alex Ross each firing a 71. McNamara and Hagen, the Americans, were right behind at 73. Vardon, 75, and Ray, 79, were still in the picture, too. After the day's second round, Vardon and Wilfred Reid led all golfers with a 147. Ray was second, at 149. After three rounds, Ouimet emerged and found himself tied with Vardon and Ray for the lead, at 225.

Five holes into the fourth round, Ouimet knew what he must do to win. Ray and Vardon had both finished with 79s and Hagen had self-destructed on the back nine, leaving a tiny opening for Ouimet. He started badly, however, scoring a 43 on the front nine, then losing two more strokes to par on the tenth hole. Ouimet struggled along playing par golf until the seventeenth, when he dropped a beautiful iron shot approximately fifteen feet from the hole. His putt was strong but true. He was tied with Vardon and Ray with one hole to play. Unfortunately, a second birdie was not in the cards. Ouimet registered a routine par on the eighteenth to force a playoff with the two British giants.

In truth, Vardon and Ray didn't dwell on the presence of an anonymous twenty-year-old amateur. Neither did anyone else. Vardon, after all, had won the only other U.S. Open he had bothered to enter and would ultimately win the British Open an incredible six times. Ray, his genial traveling companion, had won the British Open the previous year at Muirfield, Scotland, and placed second to J. H. Taylor earlier that season at Hoylake, England. In his later years, Vardon admitted that he and Ray were concerned only with each other as the playoff began.

As they stepped to the first tee, Ouimet looked almost frail compared to the two older, stockier British golfers. The head of

Ouimet's ten-year-old caddy, Eddie Lowery, barely reached the middle of Ouimet's chest; together they looked like two boys among men. Yet Ouimet refused to be intimidated. When he dropped his first putt, a ticklish five-footer, he seemed to convince himself that he might hold his own. In addition, the crowd, which would swell somewhere past 10,000, loved it.

Experience is a wonderful resource, but youth can be an advantage, too. Vardon had always been an erratic putter, and on this day it became obvious that the nerveless Ouimet had the best touch around the greens. Through the first nine holes, the trio was even at 38, but Ouimet pulled ahead by a stroke on the tenth hole. Suddenly Vardon and Ray realized they had badly underestimated Ouimet. He added another stroke to his lead on the twelfth hole and won going away. Ouimet's 72 under immense pressure left Vardon, 77, and Ray, 78, far back in his wake. The crowd was just as thrilled as Ouimet, for they had discovered a hero.

Remember, this was a time when America wasn't overly dour and cynical. Ouimet, truly a local boy, had overcome great odds. A rank amateur, he had won the U.S. Open in his first try against seasoned professionals. Foreign professionals, at that. Ouimet's victory injected into the game of golf a powerful surge of popularity. Newspapers offered breathless accounts of the homebred's slaying of the British dragons with the national title on the line. Young Americans everywhere were moved to take up the game. Not only did Ouimet spark a huge interest in golf, he helped change the rather stiff perception that golf was a game merely for the rich. Many people across the country identified with Ouimet's humble beginnings; in the years that followed his triumph, public courses began to spring up.

It was also somehow appropriate that Ouimet never turned professional. He was the U.S. Amateur champion a year later and won that title again in 1931, after a span of seventeen years. Ouimet was involved in every Walker Cup match between 1922 and 1949, either as a player or captain. Yet it was his performance over three days in the dank weather of a New England autumn that shaped history. A challenge had been issued, a line had been crossed. Only two English golfers since that time (Ray in 1920 and Tony Jacklin in 1970) have managed to win the U.S. Open, which had once seemed the birthright of golfers from the British Empire.

Walter Hagen **(ABOVE)** *was stylish off the tee, and straight, too. His casual grace was a feature of the 1914 U.S. Open, which he won with a record-tying 290. Jerome D. Travers* **(OPPOSITE PAGE)**, *the finest amateur golfer of his time, won the 1915 U.S. Open at Baltusrol Golf Club.*

The Bettmann Archive

MIDLOTHIAN COUNTRY CLUB
BLUE ISLAND · ILLINOIS

Lost in Francis Ouimet's dazzling triumph in the 1913 U.S. Open was the first appearance of that other twenty-year-old, Walter Hagen. He had faded on the final round and shot an 80, not bad for most rookies, but Hagen was crushed. He began to see himself as a baseball player. Only an offer from a local businessman to pay his expenses to Midlothian convinced Hagen that the U.S. Open was worth another try.

He arrived in Illinois cutting a typically wide swath. Until that time the game of golf was usually played in mundane sweaters, Norfolk jackets, and breeches. Every sport has its pioneers and Hagen was golf's gate-crasher with respect to fashion. He had worn a bandana around his neck and a silk shirt at Brookline, and as golf moved into the giddy 1920s, he would set the standard with brightly colored cardigans, polka-dot bow ties, and jaunty two-tone wing tips. He could also play a little golf.

In the first round at Midlothian, Hagen displayed the golfing style that would make him a legend. He had come away from Brookline impressed with Vardon's studied casualness and had incorporated that approach into his own game. There were times when Hagen almost seemed to walk into his shots, and his wide stance caused a follow-through that approached being awkward. As a result, his tee shots were often wild. Hagen managed to compensate, however, and recovery became his specialty. His short irons to the green, the mashie (five-iron), the mashie niblick (seven-iron), and the niblick (nine-iron), usually saved him from disaster. His trusty putter often turned certain pars into birdies. Hagen opened with a 35 on the front nine, then birdied four of the last five holes. It all added up to a 68, a course record. Ouimet, however, lurked only one stroke behind. After the day's second round, Hagen led with a 142, trailed by Tom McNamara, 143, and Ouimet, 145.

After a 75 in the third round, Hagen faltered midway through the fourth. He lost three strokes on the eighth and ninth holes, while amateur Chick Evans closed within a stroke of the lead. In a shades-of-Ouimet charge, Evans could have drawn even with a short putt on the ninth, but missed. At that point, Evans' putting deserted him completely. Hagen's 73 gave him an aggregate of 290 for the tournament, tying George Sargent's record, set in 1909.

1 9 1 5

BALTUSROL GOLF CLUB
SPRINGFIELD · NEW JERSEY

The term ''amateur golfer,'' while completely accurate, did not precisely describe the champion of the 1915 Open, Jerome D. Travers of America. He was an extraordinary amateur golfer, not a duffer (the kind of amateur golfer whose divot often flies farther than his ball). Francis Ouimet and Chick Evans, also exceptional amateurs, were probably better golfers overall, but Travers was the finest amateur champion of his time. He had won the U.S. Amateur title four times by 1913, holding the record until Bobby Jones, years later, won five.

Travers began swinging golf clubs at age nine, when numerous boys were dreaming about swinging baseball bats in the major leagues. He grew up loving golf, learning golf. Alex Smith, the U.S. Open champion in 1906 and 1910, taught Travers the game and the methodology of champions. Travers won the Intercollegiate Championship in 1904 at the age of seventeen, and beat Walter J. Travis, previously the hottest amateur golfer in America, in the 1905 Metropolitan champ-

UPI/Bettmann

ionship. He won another Metropolitan title in 1906 and the U.S. Amateur in 1907 and 1908, then again in 1912 and 1913. Winning an Open someday sure did look like the natural progression for him.

His timing and the site selection were perfect in 1915, the year the Open came back to Baltusrol Golf Club near Travers' home. He shot 78 in the first round, 72 in the second, and led everybody in the field except Jim Barnes, an Englishman residing in Philadelphia, the birthplace of American independence from Great Britain.

Travers began the third round two strokes behind Barnes, but shot 73 and ended up one stroke ahead of Mike Brady, Robert McDonald, and Frenchman Louis Tellier. There was nothing more to do except decide where to rank the Open in his collection of significant national championships. At least it seemed that way until the beginning of the fourth round, when Travers lost control of his swing, heretofore his trusty golfing asset. The cannibal known as Open pressure fed freely on his lead. Travers lost four shots to par over the first seven holes and went out in 39. Then his tee ball went out of bounds at the tenth hole, he topped his drive at the eleventh, and he overshot the twelfth green.

Travers suddenly looked like a weary marathon runner staggering toward the finish line. Remarkable putting revived him, but he still needed six pars to tie for first place. He strung pars on the thirteenth and fourteenth holes. The golfing gods, usually pitiless, were lenient with him at the fifteenth hole, 462 yards of danger. Travers' second shot kissed the lip of a fairway bunker but skidded out of trouble toward the green. He got up and down from thirty feet and made four at the par-five. Travers did not unsheathe his undependable woods for the rest of the round, made three pars, shot 75, and beat luckless Tom McNamara 297 to 298.

This was Travers' last victory in a national championship. He immediately went into business on Wall Street. He was a luckier golfer than he was a businessman—when the stock market collapsed in 1929, Travers, a cotton broker, lost bales of money.

He returned to golf as a professional, but the appearance fees from some exhibition matches could not restore his fortune. Travers also sold mallet putters and Spalding Red Dot golf balls, but too few to matter.

1 9 1 6

MINIKAHDA COUNTRY CLUB
MINNEAPOLIS · MINNESOTA

Golf came as naturally as breathing to Chick Evans, the busiest amateur golfer of his time and the Open titlist in 1916.

No one struck golf balls more squarely or more consistently than Evans during his era. The fairway was his launching pad; and his brassie and spoon must have been secretly equipped with telescopic sights, because he was as accurate with them from two hundred yards and beyond as most other golfers were with their wedge.

Evans, alas, could not putt. This conspicuous imperfection in an otherwise estimable game prevented historians from chiseling his likeness onto the Mount Rushmore of exceptional golfers at the end of his career.

Posterity may ignore him, but the law of averages was his playing partner in his Open year. Evans entered so many national events (more than fifty in all) that he had to win one of them. He had been a semifinalist in four U.S. Amateurs, but had been a finalist only in 1912, when Jerome Travers pressed spike marks into Evans' pride, hammering him, seven and six.

Furthermore, since Travers, the previous Open champion, had withdrawn from competitive golf and Francis Ouimet did not enter the tournament, Evans and Walter Hagen were the favorites, re-creating their duel from the 1914 Open.

Evans, then twenty-six, did not belly flop in this driving contest, though doing so would have been an understandable response in the wet conditions. The Minikahda Club had shrunk overnight in cold rain. The result of the downpour was a soaked course, an easier course. Because the greens were softer and thus simpler to putt on during the first nine holes, Evans went out in 32 and had the field behind him, though not far enough behind to comfort him.

Evans looked in his rearview mirror and saw Wilfred Reid, who had gone out in 33, a lot closer than he had expected. The two shared the lead at the end of the first round with 70s. In the second round, Evans broke free from Reid with a 69. Reid's run at the title ended on the second nine of the third round. Again he was white-hot on the first nine, taking just

Chick Evans, the busiest amateur golfer of his era, won the 1916 U.S. Open with an aggregate score of 286, the record total until 1936.

Brown Brothers

32 shots to finish the front side. He melted on the back side, shooting 43 with three successive sevens. Evans shot an inconsistent 74 but retained his lead.

Evans began the final round four shots ahead of Reid and seven in front of Jock Hutchison. Reid disappeared faster than rain water in the summer heat, but Hutchison, playing five holes behind the leader, charged at Evans with a 68. He finished at 288, breaking the Open record of 290 set in 1909.

Feeling the heat from the searing sun and Hutchison, Evans challenged the longest hole at Minikahda—the thirteenth, 525 yards of risk and peril. A creek bisecting the fairway increased the degree of difficulty. Most players had laid up ahead of the

wicked water hole with their second shots—better to be safe than soggy, after all. Evans evidently felt strong and emboldened when he reached his drive, because he told a friend, "I think I can afford to take a chance."

His ball lay some 210 yards from the cup. Undaunted, Evans swung, launching the ball toward the flag, and watched it clear the creek and land on the green. Evans was drawing close to winning the Open, a title he had lost by one infuriating stroke to Hagen two years before. With two putts he had his birdie and the momentum he needed to ice the victory and freeze out Hutchison. A 73 left him with an aggregate score of 286, the Open record for twenty years.

1 9 1 9

BRAE BURN COUNTRY CLUB
WEST NEWTON · MASSACHUSETTS

The USGA pushed the pause button on the Open in 1917 and 1918. America waited until the end of World War I to resume its championship.

The tournament looked different when it returned: the purse had grown almost three times its old size to $1,745, and the length of the championship had been extended from two days to three. The number of money winners also stretched to twelve. The only thing familiar about the event was the champion: Walter Hagen, the winner in 1914 and suddenly the best golfer in the country.

"The Haig" gave professionals legitimacy and publicity. He was the Great Gatsby of golf: extravagant, pompous, and care-free. Hagen did not look or act like the son of a blacksmith from Rochester, New York. He wore silk shirts, silk ties, vivid argyles, crisp trousers, alpaca sweaters, saddle shoes, and gold cuff links to work. There was enough oil on his hair to lubricate scores of automobile chassis. He ate vichyssoise and roast duck and drank champagne at lunch, then went out and regularly won another tournament or exhibition match.

Deciphering Hagen was no easier than defeating him. He was so unpredictable—intensely competitive one day and equally indifferent on other occasions. He was also the master of match play, and a despicable and able gamesman. He frequently used his ample powers of psychology to intimidate his competition. Hagen would often deject and confuse his opponents by strutting to their bags uninvited, inspecting their clubs, shaking his head sorrowfully, and swaggering back to his own bag.

His confidence and presence were often enough to disarm an opponent without a struggle.

Believing himself unbeatable petrified some of his opponents and helped Hagen build his impressive record and

Flamboyant Walter Hagen (OPPOSITE PAGE), *the 1919 Open titlist, gave professional golfers publicity and legitimacy.*

reputation. Mike Brady probably lost his nerve and all of his comfortable lead in the 1919 Open because Hagen was chasing him. Through the first three rounds Brady averaged about 74, always respectable golf then and more so in the Open. His total, 221, was five shots better than Hagen's. When Brady shot an 80 in the fourth round, however, he wobbled into the clubhouse with thoughts of defeat plaguing him.

No one on the course was conceding the title to Hagen—especially because he needed to shoot par on the back nine to tie Brady. The odds did not favor his chances of adding another Open pelt to his trophy room when he hooked his drive out of bounds at the eleventh hole, costing him a bogey. He retrieved the lost stroke with a birdie at the thirteenth hole and had an opportunity to finish off Brady at the eighteenth. His second shot at the seventy-second hole lay eight feet from the cup—eight feet from another birdie and another victory.

Hagen, always theatrical, sensed victory. Acting like a smug matador about to plunge the final sword into the neck of a dying bull, he dispatched someone to alert Brady of his imminent arrival at the green. Brady came out of the clubhouse. Hagen lined up the putt. He stroked the ball toward the middle of the hole. The ball orbited the rim of the cup, but did not fall.

Hagen and Brady tied for first at 301.

The following day Hagen won the playoff 77 to 78, as much through resourcefulness as through skill. He led Brady by two shots with two holes remaining in the championship round. But when his tee ball at the seventeenth swerved off line and sunk several inches in a long strip of slop, Hagen appeared to be vulnerable. He sought relief, claiming a spectator must have accidentally ground the ball far into the muck with a shoe. Officials disagreed with him, but Hagen, thinking quick on his cleats, demanded to identify his ball, his right under the rigid rules of golf.

Hagen freed the ball from its muddy morass and expertly replaced it without its resinking. He wound up making five, losing only one shot of his lead, and won the title with a par on the eighteenth hole.

When Hagen was serious he was one of the great golfers of his era. He won eleven major championships (five PGAs, four British Opens, and two U.S. Opens), a record until Jack Nicklaus won his twelfth two generations later.

Brown Brothers

INVERNESS CLUB
TOLEDO · OHIO

Harry Vardon came to the Inverness Club playing the back nine of his illustrious career; indeed, Inverness was one of the stops on his farewell tour of America. He was traveling from club to club in the East and Midwest, taking bows, accepting tributes, and regularly winning matches with his partner and close friend, Ted Ray. Vardon, then fifty, nearly left Ohio with an elegant going-away present: his second U.S. Open title. But in 1920, Ray was the Open survivor by one shot.

Jock Hutchison shot 69 in the morning round, 76 in the afternoon round, and led the tournament at the end of thirty-six holes by a thin margin. Jim Barnes, the winner of the first two PGA championships, and Leo Diegel, all of twenty-one, were merely one shot behind Hutchison, the runner-up in the 1916 Open at Minikahda. An imposing trio—Vardon, Ray, and the defending champion, Walter Hagen—were two strokes back at 147. Hagen shot 41 on the front nine of the third round and lost his chance to repeat as Open champion. Vardon appeared to be following Hagen to the slaughterhouse when he butchered the first hole. Vardon mishit his first two shots pitifully. He then needed three putts from ten feet to finish the hole; his second putt missed from eighteen inches.

Vardon was one of those people who refuse to age without battling nature and challenging stereotypes. The consequences of aging were ambushing him daily, but, even though he had lost his putting touch, an almighty golfing commodity, he did not surrender to time or concede defeat to the field.

Although he began the third round scrawling an ugly six on his scorecard, Vardon wound up approving a beautiful 71 and led Diegel and Hutchison by one stroke, and Ray by two, going into the fourth round. Vardon, the first Open champion of the twentieth century and the runner-up in 1913, went out in 36 and needed only to duplicate that average score to add another title to his outstanding list of accomplishments, which also included six British Open championships. When he made par on the tenth hole and birdie at the eleventh, Vardon led by four shots with seven holes to play. Vardon seemingly had enough distance between himself and his opponents to coast to victory. The U.S. Open, however, annually tests what the best golfers on Earth have in their tank and Vardon's gas gauge rapidly approached "empty" somewhere around the twelfth hole, the longest hole on the course. A panting wind prevented him from reaching the faraway twelfth green in regulation, even with three solid shots. He made six on that hole and lost one stroke of his lead.

In the end, Vardon did not have enough reserve energy, power, or composure to reach the finish line ahead of the competition. In fact, several able golfers lost their nerve during the 1920 Open, enabling Ray to scale the pile of bodies of prospective champions and ascend to the top of the leaderboard. Vardon jabbed awkwardly at his par putt from two feet at the thirteenth hole and left the green scoring another bogey on his scorecard. He went on to score bogeys on the fourteenth, fifteenth, and sixteenth holes. Vardon, who three-putted three consecutive greens and shot 42 coming in and 78 overall, finally broke his string of bogeys at the seventeenth hole— with a double bogey 6.

An immaterial par at the eighteenth hole was more painful than helpful; his four there left him one shot behind Ray, who at forty-three years of age became the oldest Open champion until Ray Floyd won in 1986. Vardon was also tied for second with Jack Burke, Jr., Diegel, and Hutchison. All four shot 296. Vardon went home to England without another souvenir from America.

1 9 2 1

COLUMBIA COUNTRY CLUB
CHEVY CHASE · MARYLAND

This tournament was no contest. Jim Barnes ran the table at the 1921 Open. Barnes, who had unsuccessfully stalked the title in the past, shot 69, 75, 73, 72 for a total of 289, led every round, and beat Walter Hagen and Fred McLeod by nine shots.

The cut-and-dried 1921 Open contained an important subtext: the beginning of the Bobby Jones' saga.

Jones' taxiing into history was all but lost in Barnes' exhaust fumes. There were 14 strokes separating Jones and Barnes,

Ted Ray (OPPOSITE PAGE) of Great Britain beat his best friend Harry Vardon, and the remainder of the field, at the 1920 U.S. Open. Jim Barnes (ABOVE) led from start to finish at the 1921 U.S. Open at Columbia Country Club in Chevy Chase, Maryland.

which was too many to please Jones, then too young and too proud to accept defeat graciously. Golfing on a treadmill probably annoyed the nineteen-year-old Jones more than losing. He had made no progress in the standings in one year, finishing fifth again, at the age of nineteen.

Although he was barely old enough to drive anything other than a golf ball, Jones was among the best shotmakers in the United States, perhaps in the world. But he did not yet know how to manage his estimable game and skills. Like most teenagers, Jones considered himself bulletproof. He often attempted impulsive shots, enjoying the risk as much as the success. Jones might have beaten the sacred tag team of Ted Ray and Harry Vardon at the 1920 Open if he had been more of a golfer than a daredevil that year. He shot 78 in the first round of that Open, but recovered and trailed Vardon by only four shots at the end of fifty-four holes. A 70 in the fourth round would be his lucky number, Jones thought at lunch. He was as disappointed as any lottery loser when he shot 77 and realized afterward that 72 would have been the winning number against Ray, who went around in 295, four strokes fewer than Jones.

Jones lost because he took too many risks, the result of his own impetuousness and pressure from the situation. He had come to the Columbia Country Club in 1921 full of promise and expectations. He started with another 78 and climbed into third with a 71, but 77s in the third and fourth rounds left him frustrated and in fifth place.

He was on course to fulfill his dreams and potential, but first "Unbeatable" Bobby Jones had to learn how to control his game and emotions and tolerate yet another loss.

1 9 2 2

SKOKIE COUNTRY CLUB
GLENCOE · ILLINOIS

One gets the feeling that Bobby Jones, full of youthful energy and impatience, did not stop to think that even da Vinci colored outside the lines when he was younger. Failure drove Jones more than success. He had won some important regional tour-

Gene Sarazen (OPPOSITE PAGE) *shot 68 in the fourth round and, at the age of twenty, barely beat Bobby Jones at the 1922 Open.*

naments—the Georgia Amateur at age fourteen and the Southern Amateur twice, at ages eighteen and twenty—but he had yet to finish first in a national championship. The omission of such an accomplishment from his growing portfolio of titles irritated him, even at the age of twenty.

Leg surgery early in the year did not seem to affect him or alter his goal of winning the 1922 U.S. Open, and he went into the tournament hotter than the sands of the Sahara at noon. He led the tournament at the end of three rounds, but had company in first place. He unexpectedly shared the lead with Wild Bill Melhorn, a fabulous ballstriker and a jittery putter.

Jones and Melhorn were as different as birdie and bogey. Jones looked something like a human Jumbo Ozaki driver: long, slender, with an oversize head. Melhorn looked as if someone had turned him upside down until all the muscle in his body settled in his forty-four-inch chest.

Melhorn, though built like an ox, did not look like much of an obstacle to Jones, who was determined to leave the Skokie Country Club with the Open trophy. A reputation for unraveling during the critical rounds of national tournaments unfairly followed Jones from hole to hole, dogging him even more closely than his caddie. "That Jones boy has everything," he heard in clubhouses and locker rooms at prestigious courses across the country. "But he can't go in the clutch."

After fifty-four holes, Jones had snipped two strokes per round from his scores, starting with 74, and figured he could not lose if he continued that progression by scoring 68 in the final round. It turned out that Jones was an even better swami than he was a golfer. His personal prediction was 100 percent correct. He made just one significant miscalculation: he did not count on Gene Sarazen, an assistant club professional from New York, shooting the winning score.

Sarazen, also twenty, had been hiding in the pack; he shot 72 and 73 the first day, and made birdies on three of the last five holes in the third round for a score of 75. Melhorn, the first of the leaders to tee off, shot 38 on the front nine, 74 overall, and anxiously went to the clubhouse with his 290 total. Sarazen went out in 33 and suddenly had momentum and the con-

FPG International

vivial gallery behind him. Although he made a bogey at the tenth hole, Sarazen overcame the error with birdies at the twelfth and thirteenth.

He went to the eighteenth green, 485 yards long, thinking par. When he split the fairway with a prodigious drive, Sarazen rethought his strategy at the par-five hole. The green was reachable in two shots, but Sarazen had to decide whether or not the headwind was too strong. Champions tend to be more courageous than cautious, and Sarazen was no exception—he drew his driver from his bag. His lie was perfect, as was his contact with the ball. The cannon shot landed on the edge of the

green, bounced once, and stopped rolling fifteen feet from the cup. A spectacular birdie and an aggregate of 288 were his awards for such heroism.

Jones was the sole golfer in the field capable of catching Sarazen. He shot 36 on the first nine and abandoned thoughts of coming in at 68. Tying Sarazen, however, would require only ordinary golf, another 36. But untimely bogies at the tenth, twelfth, and seventeenth holes, the latter the result of bad luck more than a poor swing, did Jones in. He lost by one troublesome stroke. He had to share second place with a grandfather, John Black, and bear another close loss.

1 9 2 3

INWOOD COUNTRY CLUB
INWOOD · NEW YORK

Bobby Jones understood more than the tricky mechanics of golf; he also understood the mystery and misery of this equally intricate and tantalizing sport. "On the golf course," he once wrote, "a man may be the dogged victim of inexorable fate, be struck down by an appalling stroke of tragedy, become the hero of unbelievable melodrama, or the clown in a side-splitting comedy—any of these within a few hours, and all without having to bury a corpse or repair a tangled personality."

Jones philosophized about the game as well as he played it. He was the best golfer of his time, and among the best of all time. He was an amateur his entire career and essentially a weekend golfer, but he won thirteen national titles in eight years.

Jones' swing was as economical as it was flawless and his game was so well balanced that observers disagreed about which part of it was most remarkable. He did not bloody his

hands pounding the ball the way a young Lee Trevino did many years later on scrubby courses in Texas. Instead, Jones' game was so graceful and seemed to come to him so instinctively that it is difficult to believe that he had once dreamed of being a professional baseball player.

Jones' prime was brief—eight years—and he was never the sort of golfer to monomaniacally travel from tournament to tournament in order to perfect his game, but he was undeniably of champion stock. His record in national championships, initially terrible, was incredible from 1922 to 1927: of seventeen such events, he finished either second or first in all but four.

Winning the Open in 1923 did not seem to be Jones' destiny. He came to the Inwood Country Club, after all, without an essential tool: confidence. Successful golfers need confidence more than spotless clubs. Failure in three previous Opens had unsettled him and worse, he had begun playing scattershot golf, spraying tee shots so regularly he barely broke 80 in practice rounds.

When the tournament began, though, Jones found his missing confidence and swing on the course, shooting 71 and

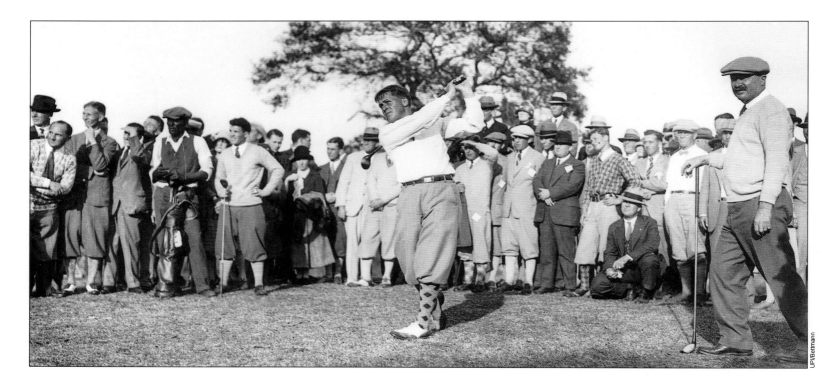

UPI/Bettmann

73 in the first two rounds. Jock Hutchison, who frequently led in the beginning rounds of the Open, led Jones by two shots at the end of 36 holes, but Jones and Bobby Cruickshank, 145, had Hutchison in their cross hairs. Hutchison shot himself from the tournament with an 82 in the third round. Jones' 76 put him in the lead, three shots ahead of Cruickshank and four ahead of Hutchison. One more average round and Jones would be the Open champion at last, at the age of twenty-one.

Jones pitted himself against Cruickshank instead of par at the outset of the fourth round and lost his concentration; he went out in 39. A 35 on the second nine would add up to a winning score of 74, Jones thought, and since he had not shot more than 35 on the incoming nine in three previous rounds, Jones began celebrating in his mind. The "victory ceremony" began with an 18-foot birdie putt at the tenth hole and a 10-foot par putt at the eleventh. Pars at the twelfth and thirteenth holes, another birdie at the fourteenth hole, and another exceptional par at the fifteenth hole left him two under par and approaching victory at maximum speed. Three pars separated Jones from the title, a flimsy barrier considering he had twice finished 4-4-3 on the final three holes, all par-fours. Unfortunately, disaster followed him to the winner's circle. Instead of breezing to victory, Jones wheezed all the way to the clubhouse. He bogied the sixteenth and seventeenth holes and double-bogied the eighteenth, to limp in with 76 for a total of 296. "I didn't finish like a champion," he told his friend O. B. Keeler of the *Atlanta Journal*, "I finished like a yellow dog."

Cruickshank had an opportunity to win the Open, and further frustrate Jones, until he made bogey at the thirteenth and fifteenth holes and double bogey at the sixteenth. A miracle birdie from six feet at the eighteenth hole saved him the same total as Jones.

The two men came to the final hole of the playoff tied. Cruickshank hooked his tee shot onto a snaking road that wound through the course. Jones outdrove Cruickshank by 100 yards, but his ball landed on a patch of bare earth in the right rough. Cruickshank's pitch shot nicked some overhanging leaves and died 50 yards short of a moat protecting the green.

Jones, 190 yards from the green and victory, now had to decide whether to lay up safely or challenge himself and the merciless golfing gods. If he did not strike the ball cleanly, it

AP/Wide World Photos

Bobby Jones (OPPOSITE PAGE) *finally won the Open at the age of twenty-one, with one of the most memorable approach shots in golf history. Cyril Walker* (ABOVE), *a lightweight among golfing heavyweights, somehow won the 1924 U.S. Open at Oakland Hills Country Club in Birmingham, Michigan.*

© David Cannon/Allsport

would probably sink in the moat and drown his chances of beating Cruickshank. He strode to the ball confidently, yanked a mid-iron from his bag, peered at the green ahead of him, and swung.

He launched both the ball and himself into golf history.

The ball landed lightly on the green and rolled six feet past the cup. The shot unnerved Cruickshank, who overshot the green with his second pitch and made six for 78. Jones' easy four gave him a 76 and the title he had sought since adolescence.

1 9 2 4

OAKLAND HILLS COUNTRY CLUB
BIRMINGHAM · MICHIGAN

One thing that makes the U.S. Open interesting is that sometimes the favorites lose to someone anonymous, someone whom the sneering golfing gods use to taunt the Joneses, Hagens, Sarazens, Nicklauses, Palmers, Hogans, Watsons, and Irwins. How else can we explain Cyril Walker's victory in 1924? The smallest golfer in the field slew the monster known as Oakland Hills and at the same time plowed through a field that included Bobby Jones, Walter Hagen, Bobby Cruickshank, and Gene Sarazen.

Walker, at 118 pounds, was a lightweight in a group of golfing heavyweights. His credentials—twice runner-up to Hagen in the North and South Open and victor against Sarazen in an early round of the 1921 PGA Championship—were neither imposing nor clues to his prospects of success.

He shot successive 74s in the first day of the tournament and trailed no one other than Jones and Wild Bill Melhorn, who topped the leaderboard at 147. Walker caught Jones with another 74 in the third round; he and Jones were unlikely duelists for the Open title. Walker shot 38 on the front nine and grew more confident with each shot. Par at the tenth hole, Jones' nemesis throughout the tournament, elated Walker even more when someone told him Jones had begun 6-4-5-4.

In 1924, Oakland Hills was a modern golf course that seemed like it had been stretched on the rack—it was 6,880 yards long. The tenth hole, 440 yards of peril, surely must have been unconstitutional at the time. A hole tough enough to frazzle Jones could not have been legal. Golfing geniuses expect to make three at such holes, and surely no more than four. But Jones, chasing his second Open title in succession, made three sixes and one five in four rounds at the tenth hole. The uncharacteristic errors there cost Jones the chance to defend his title.

Walker won the Open pot with a gambling shot at the sixteenth hole, another menacing par-four. He hit a good drive, but faced a difficult decision and approach shot. His cautious caddie wanted Walker to use a driving iron to assure himself of clearing the creek bisecting the fairway. Walker chose a mid-iron. His judgment was as good as the shot he played. The ball soared over the wicked water hole, plopped on the green and stopped eight feet from the hole. Walker lagged his first putt, tapped in his second, and left the hole with a par and an improbable victory.

1 9 2 5

WORCESTER COUNTRY CLUB
WORCESTER · MASSACHUSETTS

By now, the U.S. Open had become Bobby Jones' personal platform. He had turned twenty-three only two months before the biggest Open field in history began qualifying for the Worcester tournament, but his fingerprints were all over the three previous championships. Jones had tied for second, a stroke behind 1922 winner Gene Sarazen at Skokie, he had won the next year at Inwood, and been the runner-up to Cyril Walker the year before at Oakland Hills. Jones, of course, was the overwhelming favorite in 1925. Willie MacFarlane's name rarely came up in pre-tournament discussions.

MacFarlane had something of an off-center personality. At times, the Scotsman displayed a lovely, almost artistic game, but tenacity was not a word in his vocabulary. Though he routinely burned up courses on the New York state circuit, his appearances in the U.S. Open were as streaky as his golf. MacFarlane hadn't played in the national championship for five years when he teed off at Worcester. After Jones opened with

Willie MacFarlane (ABOVE) *did not have the nerves of steel that most U.S. Open champions possess, but he did play an artful game.*
OPPOSITE PAGE: *Oakland Hills as it looked in 1985.*

UPI/Bettmann

a dismal (for him) 77, however, it was anyone's tournament. MacFarlane became a factor after the second round when he found his peculiar rhythm and fired a 67. That eclipsed the record of 68 set by Dave Hunter in 1909.

By the fourth round, it seemed everyone of substance was in contention. Former champions Walter Hagen and Francis Ouimet, for instance, were in it until the last hole. Eventually, the field of possible champions was narrowed down to Jones and MacFarlane. Jones had recovered brilliantly, shooting 70, 70, and 74. MacFarlane, who made the final turn three strokes ahead of Jones, wilted under pressure and wound up tied with Jones at 291. In the eighteen-hole playoff MacFarlane found himself putting for the championship but missed a six-foot putt on the final hole. That left Jones and MacFarlane deadlocked at 75, so they played another eighteen. This time, inexplicably, it was Jones who faltered down the stretch. He enjoyed a four-stroke lead on MacFarlane at the turn, but MacFarlane's 33 for the back nine gave him a one-stroke victory over Jones, who stumbled home with a 38.

1 9 2 6

SCIOTO COUNTRY CLUB
COLUMBUS · OHIO

As brilliant as he was, Jones had shown a certain lack of grit in his four previous U.S. Opens. Sure, he was in the money every time, but three second-place finishes left some observers wondering if he had the stuff of legends. Jones set about reestablishing himself at the championship level with a come-from-behind victory in the 1926 British Open at Royal Lytham. He arrived back in the United States and started at Scioto with a sterling 70. In retrospect, that opening round was probably fashioned purely on adrenaline. For Jones had rushed back from Britain by ship and train and was exhausted when he reached Ohio. Even the USGA's new three-day format, calling for one round each of the first two days, followed by two rounds on the third day, offered Jones no relief. His second round of 79 betrayed a lack of rest; it was the worst round he would ever play in a U.S. Open.

After recovering with a 71 in the third round, Jones was back in the tournament, trailing Joe Turnesa by three strokes with eighteen holes to play. Turnesa didn't wilt, though. Through eleven holes he actually led the favorite by four strokes. One hole later the lead was down to two strokes. Jones, playing behind Turnesa, registered a birdie, just as Turnesa was bogeying the twelfth hole. From that point, Jones settled down and ran off a string of pars. Turnesa, meanwhile, slowly crumbled. He lost three strokes to par and trailed Jones by a stroke going to the last hole. Somehow, Turnesa found the strength to birdie the hole and take a share of the lead.

Could Jones match that feat? The final hole at Scioto was a fairly short par-five and Jones reached it easily in two shots. His second putt gave him a round of 73 and he was the champion again. In five consecutive years, Jones had finished first or second in the U.S. Open, a remarkable achievement. At the same time, Jones earned some historic recognition: in that thirtieth national championship, Jones became the first man to win the U.S. Open and the British Open in the same year.

1 9 2 7

OAKMONT COUNTRY CLUB
OAKMONT · PENNSYLVANIA

As the golfers from both sides of the Atlantic raised their golfing skills to new levels, the USGA always managed to stay one step ahead. The classic testing courses they chose for the Open each year were the best the United States had to offer, and the USGA always had the greens at their worst for the world's finest professional golfers. Scores had been coming down for some time, but they dropped dramatically after Francis Ouimet's celebrated victory in 1913 at Brookline. His winning total was 304, but nine years later Gene Sarazen set the aggregate record of 288 and winners began scoring consistently in the 290s.

Oakmont, however, was not going to surrender easily. The course played 6,915 yards long and its greens were like glass. Even Jones couldn't master the wicked circuit. Two combatants from the British Empire, Scotland's Tommy Armour and

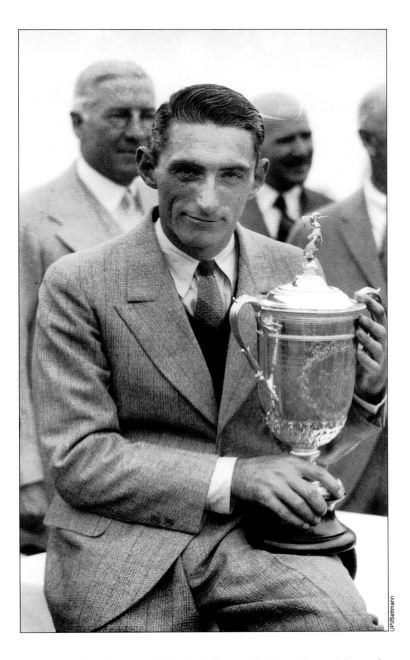

UPI/Bettmann

OPPOSITE PAGE: *Finally, in his fifth U.S. Open, Bobby Jones delivered on his immense promise. In 1926 he proved he wasn't a perpetual runner-up with a final-round 73 at Scioto Country Club in Columbus.* ABOVE: *That smug, satisfied grin belongs to 1927 U.S. Open champion Tommy Armour, whose total of 301 was the highest in modern history.*

In 1928, Bobby Jones (OPPOSITE PAGE), blasting out a bunker at Augusta National during a practice round, was the odds-on favorite at Olympia Fields Country Club in Mateson, Illinois. Despite amassing a seven-stroke lead through two rounds, however, he ultimately lost the title to the steady Johnny Farrell (RIGHT).

Johnny Farrell

England's Harry Cooper, were left flailing away at the course in the closing holes. Armour, who played out of the Congressional Country Club in Washington, D.C., had no depth perception; he had lost an eye in World War I. Cooper was already in the clubhouse at 301, when Armour made up two strokes on the six difficult closing holes to tie him.

Cooper folded in the playoff, ballooning to a 79, his worst round of the tournament. Armour put together a credible round of 76 for the victory, his first in a major championship. While Cooper would never taste that kind of success, Armour would win the British Open four years later to secure a career of distinction. The real winner that year was the golf course, though. That 301 for four rounds remains the highest shot total in modern times.

1 9 2 8

OLYMPIA FIELDS COUNTRY CLUB
MATESON · ILLINOIS

Since 1922, most U.S. Open followers had eyes only for Bobby Jones, the emerging young amateur from Georgia. During his championship reign, a handful of professionals managed to wrest the U.S. Open title away from Jones: Gene Sarazen in 1922, Cyril Walker in 1924, Willie MacFarlane in 1925, and Tommy Armour in 1927. In 1928, Johnny Farrell added his name to the list.

He was a solid player who was often overlooked. His championship record was exemplary; very quietly, while Jones was making headlines, Farrell was a model of consistency, never finishing worse than seventh in the previous five U.S. Opens. The two golfers, separated by only one year, would emerge from the largest championship field (1,064 entrants) in history.

After the first two rounds, Jones led Farrell by seven strokes. Farrell shaved off two strokes with a muscular 71, then came back with a 72 in the afternoon while Jones limped in with a 77. Once again, the U.S. Open would be decided by a playoff. Never an organization to let golfers off easily, the USGA insisted, for the first time, that thirty-six holes, not a mere eighteen, determine its champion.

Farrell broke through at the end of the first extra round with four birdies in a row to go up on Jones by three strokes. Then nerves gripped the underdog: Farrell's putting skill left him and after the first two holes of the final eighteen the match was even. Jones took a bogey on the sixteenth hole, but dropped a long putt on the seventeenth for a birdie. Farrell led by a single stroke with one hole to play. Surely, the partisan gallery thought, Jones will find an answer. Sure enough, Farrell was wild off the tee and Jones was safely on the green in two shots. Then, just when it looked like Jones would force another playoff, Farrell pitched to within ten feet of the hole and calmly dropped his birdie putt in the cup for a 143 total, one stroke ahead of Jones.

Jones took the loss well. As it turned out, he would never lose another bid for the Open trophy.

1 9 2 9

WINGED FOOT GOLF CLUB
MAMARONECK · NEW YORK

The professionals came to Winged Foot in 1929 curious to see what kind of course A. W. Tillinghast had wrought. Also the designer at Baltusrol Golf Club in nearby New Jersey, Tillinghast built the monstrous Long Island course in 1923 with the idea of challenging a golfer's mind. The wicked 180-yard, par-three tenth hole, for instance, was guarded by three traps in front and an out-of-bounds stake in back. The undulating green offered few chances for birdie. The rest of the course was harrowingly long, particularly the closing five holes, from the 417-yard fifteenth to the 452-yard sixteenth.

For these and other reasons, Winged Foot was the choice for the 1929 U.S. Open, the first of four national championships played on the course. After starting slowly, Bobby Jones, ever the favorite, tore up Tillinghast's course with a blazing 69. His 75 the next day was a small dose of Winged Foot reality before an impressive third-round 71. Nor was Jones completely alone: with

eighteen holes to play, Gene Sarazen, who had edged him seven years earlier at Skokie Country Club, lurked just four strokes behind and Al Espinosa was only a shot behind him.

When Sarazen disappeared early and Espinosa opened with an ill-advised 38 on the front nine, it seemed Jones would coast to his third U.S. Open victory. Then Espinosa settled down and went on to post a 74 for a total of 294, good enough to give him the lead in the clubhouse. Jones, meanwhile, was struggling. He posted a pair of unlucky sevens on the eighth and fifteenth holes and his lead dropped to a single shot, no safe margin considering the brutal par-fours that lay ahead. Jones drove the sixteenth hole well enough, but three-putted to fall back into a tie. The seventeenth posed no problems, but on the eighteenth the rough snared his ball on the way to the green. His chip came to rest twelve feet from the hole and now Jones needed the difficult putt to force a playoff. Confidently, he stroked the ball and it fell into the cup.

If there was any weakness in Jones' superb game, it appeared to be in the crucible of the U.S. Open playoffs. There had been the thirty-six hole loss to Willie MacFarlane in 1925 and the devastating thirty-six-hole defeat at the hands of

Johnny Farrell in 1928. This time, however, Jones never faltered He fired a sparkling 72 in the first extra round, while Espinosa, unaccustomed to the intense pressure, came in with a horrific 84. Jones closed with an emphatic 69 to win by a staggering twenty-three strokes. Could Jones possibly do anything to top that?

1 9 3 0

INTERLACHEN COUNTRY CLUB
MINNEAPOLIS · MINNESOTA

The high spirit of the 1920s was giving way to the sobering reality of the 1930s. On Valentine's Day in 1929, gangsters had killed seven rivals in Chicago. Later that year Albert Fall, the former Secretary of the Interior, was convicted of accepting a $100,000 bribe in the leasing of the Elk Hills naval oil reserve. The Teapot Dome scandal underlined a growing cynicism in the United States regarding politicians. When the bottom fell out of the stock market on October 29, that cynicism congealed into bare pessimism. Stock losses over the next three years would be estimated at fifty billion dollars. The worst economic depression in U.S. history had begun.

It was against this backdrop that Bobby Jones blazed into the nation's consciousness. His dashing good looks and astonishing grace appealed to Americans at a time when heroes were scarce. Unlike the professionals of the day, Jones had stoutly refused to accept money for his golfing exploits. He had a certain balance in his life that others envied. His wife and three children came first, followed, in order, by his Atlanta law firm, then golf. He had always maintained that perspective, but friends privately wondered what Jones might accomplish if he gave himself fully to golf, even briefly.

For several years, Jones had contemplated just that. His goal in 1930 was an unprecedented sweep of the four national championships, the U.S. Open and Amateur and the British Open and Amateur. Jones had never played much in preparation for the major events, but this year he forced himself to hone his game in time for the British Amateur, the first of the so-called Grand Slam events. Jones, who had already won two British Opens, was revered and adored by the galleries across the

OPPOSITE PAGE: *After losing the 1928 U.S. Open, Bobby Jones, at left in this unlikely foursome, won the 1929 tournament, besting Al Espinosa in the thirty-six-hole playoff.* ABOVE: *By 1930, Bobby Jones transcended golf in America. He won the U.S. Open that year and eventually completed his celebrated Grand Slam. Then, at the age of twenty-eight, he walked away from formal competition forever.*

Courtesy of Inverness Club

Atlantic. The spectators at St. Andrew's Old Course that May were behind Jones as he beat defending champion Cyril Tolley in the fourth round and Roger Wethered in the final. In avoiding several close calls, Jones had won the British Amateur for the first time and had secured the first leg of the Grand Slam.

Two weeks later, Jones won the British Open at Hoylake. His opening round of 70 equaled the course record; in the second round he came back with a 72. Jones finished with a 74 and a 75, which was just enough to edge Leo Diegel and Macdonald Smith. Lost in Jones' triumph was his declaration that Hoylake was to be his last British Open. Jones returned to the United States, where people had been keenly following his progress. Before dashing off to Minneapolis, Jones found time to ride down Broadway again and accept the plaudits and the ticker tape that were heaped on him. In a departure from past convention, Jones spent a week working on his game in some steamy practice rounds at Interlachen Country

Club. The temperature during the national championship would soar as high as 100 degrees Farenheit.

Jones' noble quest was not lost on the game's professionals. To the outside world, his success reduced them to inept, supporting characters. They were determined to stop him in the U.S. Open, the most highly visible event among the four Grand Slam competitions. Sure enough, in the first round on July 10, Macdonald Smith and Tommy Armour, two familiar rivals, scored identical 70s to take the lead. Jones, no slouch, came in at 71, along with Wiffy Cox.

On the ninth hole of the second round Jones was visited by a stroke of good fortune. The ninth hole was an imposing 484-yard par-five, but Jones had observed that by hitting a second shot over the water that ran through the middle of the hole, a birdie was possible. Jones didn't have a particularly good lie, but he aimed for the green nevertheless. Just before he moved through the ball, Jones was distracted by spectators in the gallery. Clearly, his swing was affected, for he sent a shot angling right toward the lake. Jones was looking a bogey in the face when the ball bounced off the water like it was asphalt. It came to rest thirty-odd yards from the green. Jones, still a little shaken, managed a nifty pitch and a short putt for birdie. Through nine holes he had taken only 34 strokes, one of them a wondrous act of nature. Though he faded on the back nine with a 39, Jones was only two shots behind front-runner Horton Smith. Of course, half the field seemed in the running at the tournament's midpoint.

Then, Jones took off. After the sixteenth hole of that third round, Jones was an incredible six strokes under par. He had stolen three birdies on the front nine and matched that total as he mowed through the back nine. With two holes to play, Jones seemed poised for a 66, the best score the U.S. Open had ever seen at that point. Instead, Jones faltered slightly and finished with a 68 in a superb effort that placed him five shots ahead of his nearest competitor, Harry Cooper.

Despite his comfortable cushion, Jones made an adventure of the final eighteen holes; it was his way. Macdonald Smith, who was far off the pace (seven shots) when the final round began, fought to within a shot of the lead when Jones stumbled badly at the start. Jones had opened up a three-shot advantage when his tee shot on the imposing seventeenth hole vanished into thin air. The seventeenth at Interlachen is a mighty 262-yard par-three. Instead of playing it safe, Jones went for the green and his shot bounced off a tree and caromed…well, no one in the gallery could say where it went, exactly. The official traveling with Jones' group ruled that the ball had entered a marshy water hazard. Jones, he said, should take a penalty stroke and drop the ball in the fairway opposite the point it had crossed the hazard, which Jones did, taking a five on the hole. There were those that argued the ball should have been ruled as lost, which would have required a daunting trip back to the tee platform. As it was, Jones collected himself and, with a birdie on the final hole, posted a blistering score of 287. Macdonald Smith, the golfer who had hounded him at the British Open, could not match that score. The best he could do was a 289, good only for second place.

Jones had captured the third leg of the Grand Slam. By now, the entire nation was watching. Meanwhile, only a few trusted friends knew that Jones had already decided that the U.S. Amateur at Merion would be his last formal competition. The pressure of performing in the blinding glare of publicity was exacting a toll on Jones, but he had enough strength left to finish his historic run with gusto. Jones weathered Merion and its full week of gripping eighteen-hole, match-play dramas. Through the suspense, he dispatched Gene Homans in the final. Bobby Jones had completed the Grand Slam, a feat never equaled before or since. Then, at the age of twenty-eight years and eight months, Jones walked away from the game that had given him such immense fame. It was no longer worth the strain and the imposition on his private life.

Jones played in his first U.S. Open in 1920 as an eighteen-year-old. In an eleven-year span, he won the tournament four times and was runner-up another four times. Jones also won five U.S. Amateur championships, to go with three British Opens and that one British Amateur title. As far ahead of the field as Jones was, he played in what might have been the deepest talent pool golf has ever seen. Walter Hagen and Gene Sarazen, of course, were his American contemporaries, and there were still a number of skilled players from the British Empire plying their trade, Macdonald Smith among them. Many gifted golfers from both sides of the Atlantic have followed, but never matched, Jones' sheer brilliance.

INVERNESS CLUB
TOLEDO · OHIO

The throne was vacant when the U.S. Open came to Toledo the following July; somehow it was appropriate that a record 144 holes were required to determine the 1931 winner, making it the longest national championship in history.

The serene beauty of the eighteenth green and the clubhouse at Inverness Club (OPPOSITE PAGE) *in Toledo, Ohio, was the unlikely backdrop for the bitter 1931 battle between George Van Elm and Billy Burke* (ABOVE).

With some of the more familiar names, like Macdonald Smith and Walter Hagen, four strokes off the lead with eighteen holes to play, a trio of relative unknowns led Inverness. George Van Elm, a thirty-year-old from California, was alone at 217, two strokes ahead of Billy Burke, a twenty-eight-year-old professional from Connecticut. Guy Paulsen, an Indiana golfer, was third at 220. And as the fourth round unfolded, the newcomers did not quail in the face of pressure.

Both Von Elm and Burke shot 36 over the first nine to distance themselves from the field. When Burke, playing well ahead, scored a 37 over the back nine, it was Von Elm's tourna-

ment to win or lose. Or, in this case, tie. Von Elm, perhaps finally sensing the importance of the day, slipped badly and lost four strokes to par. Only a birdie on the eighteenth hole prevented Burke from winning in the regulation seventy-two holes. Tied at 292, Von Elm and Burke stepped off the next day in a thirty-six-hole playoff.

Burke ran out to a two-stroke lead with a 73 in the opening round, but Von Elm closed and actually took a two-shot lead himself midway through the second round. Von Elm, in an eerily familiar turn of events, somehow fell a stroke behind and was forced to birdie the eighteenth hole to stay alive. Now the championship stretched to a fifth day and another thirty-six-hole test. The two men were separated by only a stroke after the first round, with Von Elm leading. Burke, however, scored a 71 in the second round to win the tournament by a stroke, 148 to Von Elm's 149. Burke and Von Elm quickly faded from the golfing landscape, but their grim battle had a far-reaching effect. The thought that a single shot was all that spared all participants a third thirty-six-hole playoff and a staggering 180-hole tournament, made an impression on the USGA. From that point on, all U.S. Open playoffs were contested over a more civilized eighteen holes.

Gene Sarazen won the 1932 U.S. Open with a searing final round of 66. Here, he displays the championship trophy while his wife holds the silver pitcher he won at the British Open earlier in the year.

1 9 3 2

FRESH MEADOW COUNTRY CLUB
FLUSHING · NEW YORK

When Gene Sarazen, born Gene Saraceni, won the 1922 U.S. Open at Skokie at the age of twenty, he was hailed as golf's new leading light. After all, Sarazen had become the first golfer to win the Open by breaking 70 in the final round. More importantly, perhaps, he had bested Bobby Jones, another distinguished twenty-year-old. Later that year, Sarazen won the PGA championship. While Jones' career took off in unprecedented fashion the following year, however, Sarazen's remarkable touch deserted him. He won the 1923 PGA title with the same streak of skill that had dazzled people the year before, but it would be nine agonizing years before he would win another major championship.

Not that Sarazen folded up completely. He won the Miami Open three times and played credibly in a handful of majors, placing second in the 1928 British Open and recording four near-misses in the U.S. Open as the 1920s waned. No one was more aware of these failures than Sarazen. In 1931, he vowed to correct the wild drives that had ruined his game when the pressure mounted. A new grip solved that problem. In an attempt to improve his bunker play, he developed a club that would evolve into the modern sand wedge. Armed with these new weapons, Sarazen won the 1932 British Open. He arrived back in the United States full of confidence.

Fresh Meadow, also designed by A. W. Tillinghast, was a course on which Sarazen was comfortable, since he had been the professional there from 1925 to 1931. Sarazen, mindful of the narrow, tightly bunkered greens, played cautiously the first two rounds, shooting 74 and 76. That put him five strokes behind Phil Perkins. Sarazen closed within a stroke of the lead with a 70 in the first of two rounds on the final day.

Sarazen's final round was a masterpiece; he went out in a four-birdie 32 and finished with an assertive 34. The total was a breathtaking 66, the best ever in a U.S. Open. Broken down, Sarazen's two rounds were extraordinary. He played the final twenty-eight holes in an even 100 strokes. Sarazen, a three-stroke winner over Perkins and Bobby Cruickshank, had vindicated himself. At the age of thirty, after a decade-long drought, Sarazen again was the national champion.

1 9 3 3

Today, in the age of million-dollar purses in professional golf, it is hard to imagine a time when amateur golf was king. Yet, even in the 1920s and 1930s, professional sports were just beginning to find a place in the hearts of Americans. Professional football, for instance, was viewed the way professional wrestling is viewed now. College football was pure, and for

LEFT: *One view of the fourteenth hole at the North Shore Country Club.* ABOVE: *John Goodman, an outstanding amateur golfer from Omaha, Nebraska, takes a stroll with Bing Crosby, an accomplished golfer in his own right.*

many people, more exciting. Golf (witness the support for Bobby Jones, the consummate amateur) had been much the same, but now there was a grudging acceptance of the professional game. No one knew it at the time, but 1933 would mark the last great stand of amateurs in the U.S. Open.

Johnny Goodman was only twenty-five years old but he had already carved out a niche of distinction. He had placed eleventh in the 1930 U.S. Open and made a habit of impressing in the U.S. Amateur; he had been a finalist in 1932. His opening-round 75 left him far back in the pack at North Shore, but a blazing 66, highlighted by five birdies and an eagle, moved him up in the tournament. A third-round 70 gave Goodman an imposing six-shot lead over Ralph Guldahl.

Goodman had encountered pressure in the U.S. Amateur, and so he responded marvelously, going three-under-par over the first three holes. Then he relaxed, losing the aggressive style that had led to his successful second- and third-round scores. He faded badly, crawling in with a 76, which opened the door for Guldahl, playing behind him. Predictably, Guldahl drew even and needed only a five-foot putt to force a playoff at 287. Somehow, he missed it. Goodman became the fifth, and last, amateur to win the U.S. Open.

1 9 3 4

MERION CRICKET CLUB
ARDMORE · PENNSYLVANIA

Golf is a fickle enterprise. Things can change in a heartbeat. Olin Dutra, a well-regarded professional, was well off the pace after two rounds of the 1934 Open, having followed an opening 76 with a 74. All told, eight strokes separated him from the leader. This was mildly surprising, because Dutra and his pendulum style of putting had met with success up to that point. Dutra, in fact, had beaten Frank Walsh in the final of the 1932 PGA championship at Keller Golf Club in St. Paul, Minnesota.

Dutra, despite a violent attack of stomach cramps, managed to put together a glistening 71 in the third round and followed that with a 72 late in the day. It was good, very good, for a total of 293, one better than two-time winner Gene Sarazen, who had self-destructed on Merion's testing eleventh hole, losing three strokes to par.

Olin Dutra (ABOVE), *who overcame third-round stomach cramps, mastered the greens of Merion in the 1934 U.S. Open.*

1 9 3 5

OAKMONT COUNTRY CLUB
OAKMONT · PENNSYLVANIA

Sam Parks, Jr., left Oakmont Country Club nearly sixty years ago telling a tall tale instead of another U.S. Open horror story. Parks shot 76 in the final round of the 1935 Open and won his only major championship, his only tournament of any kind.

His victory in the Open would be the golfing equivalent of an incredible fish story, except that the winning score of 299 is verifiable. Parks symbolizes one aspect of what makes the Open such a unique event. No professional sport except golf provides opportunities for mortals to compete against the aristocracy of the game and perhaps join the golfing gods in immortality.

Parks was an average professional golfer who in one week became an unlikely local hero by defeating slugger Jim Thomson and a truly nasty golf course.

Henry Fownes, an amateur architect, initially designed Oakmont in 1903 and his son, William, winner of the 1910 U.S. Amateur championship, modified it several times afterward. The Fownes' diabolical mantra and message was "A shot poorly played should be a shot irrevocably lost." Traps of all configurations and sizes were William Fownes' fiendish contribution to the landscape. Professional golfers despise sand traps— even the smallest can prove hazardous to the size of their paycheck. The infamous traps at Oakmont are the "Church Pews" on the third and fifteenth holes, a sinister series of hazards. The nickname ought to be "Death Row."

Traps were William Fownes' means of penalizing players strong enough to outdrive the original dimensions of the layout. "We still keep the penal nature of the course intact today," club pro Bob Ford says. "As players outgrow the distance to the bunkers, we just move the traps." Maintaining Oakmont as some sort of penal colony apparently was William Fownes' wish and legacy.

AP/Wide World Photos

PREVIOUS PAGE: *In one improbable week, Sam Parks, Jr.* (FOREGROUND), *went from average Joe, indeed, average pro, to U.S. Open champion with one of the highest totals in Open annals, 299. Tony Manero* (RIGHT), *whose name conjures up the image of a boxer rather than a golfer, set an Open scoring record when he won the 1936 title.*

Parks was the sole golfer to escape from the minefield the Fowneses had laid thirty-two years beforehand. He barely broke 300 and defeated Thomson by just two shots. He vanished from the top as fast as he appeared there, but with one victory Parks left his footprints on the sand traps of time.

1 9 3 6

BALTUSROL GOLF CLUB
SPRINGFIELD · NEW JERSEY

The middle of the 1930s saw new talent auditioning to succeed the previous leading men in professional golf, but few of the contenders were as durable or able as Bobby Jones or Walter Hagen. An implausible trio of golfers won the U.S. Open from 1934 through 1936, beginning with Olin Dutra.

In 1936 another chimerical entrant, Tony Manero, won the title in the most gloriously theatrical way possible: he shot 67 in the fourth round, 282 overall, and left the course with the precious trophy and the lowest score then for seventy-two holes in Open history.

The result of the tournament did not surprise anyone more than luckless Harry Cooper. Cooper, whose score of 284 beat the course and everybody but Manero, was in the clubhouse contemplating, and actually celebrating, his victory.

Cooper was going to win the Open—reparation for his sad loss to Tommy Armour in the 1927 Open at Oakmont Country Club. Cooper had led that tournament until the seventy-first hole. He did not cross the finish line first, though, because he three-putted the seventeenth green from twelve feet. Cooper made an untimely bogey and lost to Armour by three shots the following afternoon in a playoff. He must have done something in his past to offend the golfing gods, because nine years later he helplessly saw Manero snatch the handsome hood ornament—the Open trophy—from his strong grip.

Chick Evans' old Open record of 286 had withstood assaults from hundreds of golfers and numerous improvements in equipment from 1916 until 1936, the year Cooper and Manero broke the mark along with golf's equivalent of a tempestuous stallion, the Upper Course at Baltusrol Golf Club.

1 9 3 7

OAKLAND HILLS COUNTRY CLUB
BIRMINGHAM · MICHIGAN

Sam Snead found golf, his religion, while caddying at The Homestead in Hot Springs, Virginia, a resort course up the road a piece (as Southerners would say) from his house. The successor to Bobby Jones, Snead was plain folk from Virginia; he grew up playing barefoot and hustling suckers who mistook him for a hillbilly. Snead is living testimony that not every golfer learns the game on a magnificent course covered with emerald grass, eating caviar and sipping gin and tonics on the veranda of a palatial clubhouse afterward.

Snead learned all the aspects of golf, especially his sweet swing, at his folksy home course. He corrected a flaw in his grip there at the age of twenty-three, learned to hit with the driver and all of the other clubs in his bag, and went on to win eighty-one official golf tournaments, more than any other man in history.

Experts argue that Jones and Ben Hogan were better golfers, but Snead, born in 1912, the same year as Hogan, was more colorful and charismatic than either of them. Had televisions been widely available when Snead was in his prime, he, not Arnold Palmer, would have brought golf to the masses. Snead came from a period in golf history when players had talent and personalities, when golfers were quotable, combustible, and willing to kibitz with the gallery. Golf is now more popular than ever, but somehow not as amusing as it was when Snead was playing full time.

Although Denny Shute had won the PGA Championship and Byron Nelson had won the Masters, Snead was suddenly the ringmaster of the Greatest Show on Turf and the unanimous Open favorite in 1937. He shot 69 in the first round, tying the course record, and made the prognosticators look smart. Snead and Shute led the tournament, but five other golfers were merely one shot behind them. Snead fell to fifth in the second round, the result of a fitful 73. With 70 in the third round and 71 in the fourth, including an eagle at the seventy-second hole, he ended up in first place with 283, five under par and only one shot over the Open record.

The Open and Snead officially began their office romance in 1937, although it was Guldahl who successfully wooed the title that year.

Guldahl, who had begun the fourth round sharing second place with Snead, reached the tenth tee knowing what Snead had shot. Guldahl had gone out in 33, with an eagle on the eighth hole and a birdie on the ninth; a 37 on the incoming nine would be his lucky number. He lost precious ground and shots with consecutive bogeys on the tenth and eleventh holes, though. The odds of Guldahl defeating Snead suddenly were longer than typical Open rough: he would need to par the last seven holes just to tie him, an uncertainty at unpredictable Oakland Hills Country Club.

Guldahl approached the twelfth hole, 555 yards long, thinking birdie. He left the green entering exactly that on his card. Although the thirteenth hole was 400 yards shorter than the twelfth, a birdie was no easier to make there. But since the best golfers rarely miss birdie putts laying eighteen inches from the cup, Guldahl left this hole with a remarkable two. He had to work hard for par at the fourteenth hole and needed luck to match that average score at the following hole. His approach shot at the fifteenth hole was flying toward the sixteenth tee until it struck a spectator, bounded into a bunker, and stopped beside a cigar butt. Guldahl blasted the butt and the ball onto the green and saved par. He was tracking victory again. A trail of easy pars at the sixteenth, seventeenth, and eighteenth holes led him to the Open championship. He left the eighteenth green with a 69 for a total of 281, a scoring record, and the regal title of U.S. Open champion.

too few to deaden his interest in golf; certain aspects of the sport perpetually seduce golfers of every ability.

Pro golfers sometimes have imperfect lies, but they seem to lead enviable lives. Golfers work outdoors and most of them sport suntans lifeguards would envy. Their offices are plush courses, instead of colorless cubicles beside the elevator or the bathroom.

In the frolicking age of golf, when professional golfers spent their spare time calculating their scoring average instead of the future value of their IRA, the Byron Nelsons, Gene Sarazens, Ralph Guldahls, Sam Sneads, and Ben Hogans did not imitate important businessmen. At that time, professional golf was more of a game than an enormous multinational corporation. Professional golf was once about competition and accumulating trophies, adulation, and good wages, not bales of cash.

Guldahl heard the beguiling call of the temptress in the spring of 1936 and unexpectedly found his game at the True Temper Open in Detroit. He suddenly became hotter than leather seats in an open convertible exposed to the scorching summer sun. He won the Western Open in 1936 and the U.S. Open in 1937 and 1938.

In 1938, he shot 74, 70, 71, 69 for a total of 284, fought par and Cherry Hills Country Club to a standoff, beat Dick Metz by six strokes, and became only the fourth man in history to win successive Opens, joining Willie Anderson, Johnny McDermott, and Bobby Jones on the roster of rare repeat champions (a list that now includes Ben Hogan and Curtis Strange). Guldahl also won the Masters in 1939, but then again lost his game and desire. Discouraged, he left the tour soon afterward.

---

1   9   3   8

CHERRY HILLS COUNTRY CLUB
DENVER · COLORADO

Golf can be an equally exhilarating and exasperating game. Ralph Guldahl understood the baffling dichotomy of the sport. He was second at the 1933 Open and eighth one year later, but then quit the sport in 1935 because he lost his putting touch and dedication. He sold cars in Dallas for several months, but

---

1   9   3   9

PHILADELPHIA COUNTRY CLUB
PHILADELPHIA · PENNSYLVANIA

How someone loses in the Open can sometimes be more eventful and poignant than how someone else becomes the victor. To wit: the Open ought to contemplate changing its name to the One Significant Tournament Sam Snead Did Not Win. Catchy? No. Pertinent? Yes.

Ralph Guldahl won two consecutive Open championships, in 1937 and 1938, the first at Oakland Hills Country Club in Birmingham, Michigan, and the second at Cherry Hills Country Club, in Denver.

Snead is one of the greatest golfers in history—in his opinion as well as that of historians. His portfolio and trophy case are incomplete, however, because he never won the U.S. Open, although he was the favorite for about twenty years, and came close four times, first in 1937. He and the title were planning on leaving Oakland Hills Country Club together until Ralph Guldahl somehow shot 69 in the final round and jerked the championship from his hands.

Maybe the high-beam focus on him or his maddening bogey at the seventy-first hole paralyzed Snead in 1939. How else to explain his numbing finish at the Spring Mill course? Snead needed a five, a simple par, in order to go around in 283 and defeat Byron Nelson, Craig Wood, and Denny Shute by one shot. When Snead reached the tee at the eighteenth hole, he did not know his position on the leaderboard, and he did not ask anyone for it. As a result, he thought he had to gamble on the uphill hole to capture the Open jackpot.

He struck his tee shot squarely, but the disobliging golfing gods steered the ball left into some trampled rough 275 yards from the green. The safe shot would have been to advance the ball with an iron club, but Snead, who plays golf with the venturesome disposition of an old-time riverboat gambler, drew his brassie from his bag. Slammin' Sammy was going for the green and unknowingly heading for disaster. He topped his second shot. The ball rolled 165 yards into the middle of a deep, steep fairway bunker. Although merely 110 yards from the green, from his location, Snead could barely see the top of the flagstick, let alone the top of the leaderboard.

He needed a club with plenty of loft to escape from the baleful bunker. Instead of a wedge, Snead chose an eight-iron. He wanted to reach the green, not the fairway. In the life of every golfer there are inspiring moments—when the golf ball acts obligingly and loyally follows the correct trajectory and flight path, then vanishes into the cup. Snead needed such luck, but, in this instance, his ball had barely taken off when it landed four feet ahead of him in an unimaginable, unprintable, and unspeakable lie.

The ball had lodged in some fresh sod at the face of the bunker. In order to preserve victory now, Snead somehow had to get up and down from hell. He hacked at the ball with a wedge as if he were chopping at thick jungle plant life with a machete. The ball bounded seventy yards onto the upslope of another implacable trap protecting the green from assaults by the best golfers on earth. Snead, standing awkwardly on the grass outside the trap, punched his ball onto the green forty feet past the cup. Saving bogey and a share of first place would require a stroke of genius or a stroke of luck, perhaps both.

His sixth shot hit the hole, spun out, and stopped three feet away. He left his second putt short. Snead left the green seconds later in a trance, scribbling an eight onto his scorecard. Spectators grieved with him, as if they had been eyewitnesses to a horrible accident.

In the end, Nelson won the championship in double over-time. He and Wood each shot 68 in the first playoff round, eliminating Shute. Nelson then shot 70 over the second eighteen holes and beat Wood by three strokes.

How Snead lost makes this Open unforgettable, though. In his long, long career Sam Snead won more than one hundred tournaments, including three Masters (1949, 1952, 1954), one British Open (1946), and three PGA Championships (1942, 1949, 1952). Victories in those prestigious events, however, never did offset his one failure.

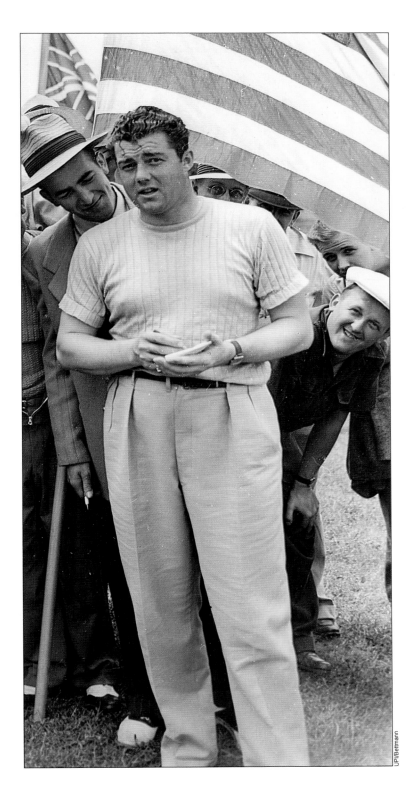

*In 1939, Byron Nelson (*OPPOSITE PAGE*) won the U.S. Open. Sam Snead lost with an incredible eight on the final hole of regulation. Lawson Little (*RIGHT*) did not dominate professional golf in the same way he did amateur golf, but he did win the 1940 U.S. Open.*

1 9 4 0

CANTERBURY GOLF CLUB
CLEVELAND · OHIO

Sam Snead shot 67 in the first round of the 1940 Open and stalked the title for fifty-four holes. He lost its scent in the final round. Snead, in second place at the beginning of the round, shot an 81, his highest Open score ever, and fell to sixteenth. But you have heard that story before.

How about this one?

Lawson Little, once the best amateur golfer since Bobby Jones, won the championship in an unlikely duel with Gene Sarazen, the Open champion in 1922 and 1932. Little, who had been playing for a living since 1937, won the U.S. and British amateurs in 1934 and 1935, so people were expecting him to excel in professional golf. Sarazen did not figure to be among the top two in the Open at age thirty-eight, which is young chronologically but almost ancient in golf years.

Little and his score of 287 sure did look safe in the clubhouse, especially since Sarazen made no headway on the first nine. He shot his age there and the longest, toughest stretch of the course lay in front of him. Catching Little meant shooting 34 on the dastardly incoming nine, not an impossibility, but an improbability. "I'll try to do it," Sarazen told friends.

A surge of adrenaline must have jolted Sarazen, because he made birdies at the eleventh and thirteenth holes and par at the next three holes, the third with a snaking putt from eight feet.

Behind him was the dangerous sixteenth hole, a serpent measuring 615 yards. Ahead of him were two more monsters: the seventeenth hole, a 230-yard par-three, and the eighteenth, a 441-yard par-four. Sarazen had made bogeys on each of those holes in the first round. He undershot the seventeenth green and pitched thirty feet short of the cup. Sarazen, who played golf with a commando mentality, did not surrender to age or pressure. He sank the putt, then launched two titanic shots toward the eighteenth hole.

Sarazen was suddenly fifty feet from the cup, fifty feet from another Open title. His birdie attempt, the game ball of sorts, stopped less than one foot from the flag. He had his 34 and

the chance to conquer age and beat Little in a playoff. What else could he need?

One more miracle.

Sarazen the magician could not conjure an encore for his previous performance from his golf bag of tricks and lost by three shots, 70 to 73. (He was luckier than disconsolate Ed "Porky" Oliver, who would have been in the playoff, too, except he was disqualified for playing out of turn in the fourth round.) Thus, Lawson Little, built more like a linebacker than a golfer, won the U.S. Open.

1 9 4 1

COLONIAL HILLS COUNTRY CLUB
FORT WORTH · TEXAS

You often need both patience and luck to win a major golfing tournament. The mischievous golfing gods often tease future champions by hinting at victory before bestowing the prestigious title on someone else. Craig Wood was a victim of such antics until 1941, his Open year.

In 1935, Wood was three shots ahead of Gene Sarazen and in the clubhouse celebrating his victory at The Masters, until Sarazen struck "The Shot." The second shot Sarazen launched flew 240 yards at the fifteenth hole of Augusta National and submerged into the hole, but has yet to stop rolling in golf lore. The double eagle alone did not do in Wood. Sarazen had to par the sixteenth, seventeenth, and eighteenth holes, and then defeat Wood in a thirty-six-hole playoff.

In 1939, Wood and Byron Nelson were mining together for the priceless nugget every serious golfer cherishes: the Open title. Wood and Nelson were even in overtime until Nelson made three on the third hole at the Philadelphia Country Club. Nelson strode to the fourth hole, 460 yards of traps and terror, one shot ahead. He struck his tee shot squarely and long, but then had trouble deciding whether to attack the flag with a wood or an iron club.

He finally chose a one-iron. The ball, as if controlled by a military computer, flew directly at the target, thumped once on the green, rolled past the hole, then reversed itself, following

In 1941, Craig Wood finally overcame the fickle golfing gods and beat Denny Shute in the last U.S. Open before the Second World War.

UPI/Bettmann

the slope of the putting surface. It lodged between the flag-stick and the rim of the cup.

The eagle, a gift from the gods, astonished everyone but Nelson. "I knew it was good when I hit it," Nelson said. "The impact was perfect. I know I had never hit a better iron." Wood had played the first four holes in even par but was three shots behind, the margin of defeat. In 1941, Wood went to Colonial Hills Country Club with a bad back and no reason to believe the gods would favor him. He made seven on the first hole, a long par-five, and had to be talked out of withdrawing. He wound up shooting 73 in the first round, and 71 in the second round. Hot, teeming rain did not shrink his desire in the third and fourth rounds. He shot 70 in both and beat Denny Shute by three strokes 281 to 284.

The U.S. Open then disappeared in the smoke and flames of World War II, and resumed in 1946.

1 9 4 6

CANTERBURY GOLF CLUB
CLEVELAND · OHIO

Six months to the day after Craig Wood had dispatched Denny Shute in the 1941 U.S. Open, the Japanese attacked Pearl Harbor. Golf suddenly became an afterthought. Many professional golfers joined the armed services and some golf courses were pressed into service. The USGA put on a brave face in 1942, and with the cooperation of the Chicago District Golf Association and the PGA, staged the Hale America Open. The June event drew some marquee names; Ben Hogan shot a 271, three strokes better than Jimmy Demaret and Mike Turnesa. According to the record book, however, the win didn't count. Otherwise, Hogan would have finished his career

APWide World Photos

with an unprecedented five Open championships. There were no U.S. Opens, formal or otherwise, over the next four years.

By the spring of 1946, much had changed in America. Harry Truman, for instance, had become president a year earlier when Franklin Roosevelt died at the age of sixty-three. Byron Nelson, who in 1944 had entered thirty-one tournaments and won eight of them, was just beginning to slide past his prime. Hogan, who oddly enough was the same age as Nelson, still had his best golf ahead of him. After a four-year hiatus, the U.S. Open returned in June 1946; a total of 1,175 golfers entered.

Nelson, who had dominated the professional tour while the war was on (he was deemed exempt from serving because his blood required almost four times as long as normal to clot), was the favorite at Canterbury. It would be, he allowed, his last U.S. Open. The rigors of the professional campaign had simply become too much. Nelson had enough gas left to make the first postwar Open a thrilling one, however. After seventy-two holes, Nelson, Lloyd Mangrum, and Vic Ghezzi were all even at 284. Nelson, alas, had bogeyed the eighteenth hole to fall into the tie.

The eighteen-hole playoff did nothing to settle the argument; all three golfers shot a 72. A second round that day would do the trick. Seemingly, this was an Open no one wanted to win. Nelson bogeyed the seventeenth hole to fall two strokes behind Mangrum, who promptly bogeyed the eighteenth. Ghezzi had a five-foot putt for par to force another eighteen-hole playoff, but he missed and Mangrum became champion.

1 9 4 7

ST. LOUIS COUNTRY CLUB
ST. LOUIS · MISSOURI

Like Byron Nelson and Ben Hogan, Sam Snead was born in 1912. Unlike Nelson and Hogan, Snead never won the U.S. Open. He had come maddeningly close in 1939, when a five on the final hole at Philadelphia Country Club would have given him the championship, but instead embarrassed himself with an eight. Snead would finish second four times in the national championship, but he would never come closer than in 1947.

In 1946, after a five-year hiatus, the U.S. Open returned to postwar America. Lloyd Mangrum (OPPOSITE PAGE), seen here teeing off at Canterbury's twelfth hole, was the eventual champion. With a tenacious final round of 69, Lew Worsham (ABOVE) ruined Sam Snead's chance for the 1947 U.S. Open trophy.

Twenty years earlier, a professional, Tommy Armour, representing the Congressional Country Club near Washington, D.C., had won the U.S. Open. It looked like history was repeating itself: Lew Worsham, the Congressional professional, opened the tournament with three sizzling rounds of 70, 70, and 71. When the twenty-nine-year-old pro shot a 33 over the front nine, the tournament seemed over. But Worsham, in time-honored fashion, began to sweat as the enormity of his achievement began to dawn on him. Worsham stumbled down the stretch, finishing with a 71 and a four-round aggregate of 282.

Snead suddenly found himself in position to win his third major championship. He took the PGA title in 1942, then added the British Open in 1946, and now, with a birdie over the last three holes, he would have another. Snead parred the

sixteenth hole at St. Louis, but bogeyed the seventeenth. Even as some in the gallery were questioning Snead's moxie, he rolled an eighteen-foot putt into the hole to force a playoff with Worsham.

The June 15 battle between Snead and Worsham made for great theater. Back and forth it went until, with one hole to play, the two golfers were dead even. Snead found the green, but Worsham's approach shot rolled into the fringe. Playing first, Worsham sent a pitch right at the hole and watched as it spun out of the cup. Now it was Snead's turn. His downhill putt from twenty feet was too cautious; it stopped a full thirty inches short of the hole. Snead moved to putt out, but Worsham asked for a ruling to see who was away. Worsham, you see, had the easier of the two putts, a slightly uphill shot,

Slammin' Sammy Snead came within thirty inches of winning the 1947 Open, but Lew Worsham took the trophy.

In the 1948 Open, Ben Hogan, a world-class champion, scored a tournament-record total of eight under par with his smooth shots.

and wanted to finish first to give Snead something to think about. Though officials determined that Worsham was marginally closer, and so must wait for Snead, doubts had begun to edge into Snead's mind. He struck the putt gingerly and the ball never had a chance; it missed by several inches and the tournament became Worsham's to win. And so he did: Worsham's 69 was a stroke better than Snead, who had been thirty inches from destiny.

1 9 4 8

RIVIERA COUNTRY CLUB
LOS ANGELES · CALIFORNIA

There had been dominant golfers before Ben Hogan terrorized the PGA tour in 1948. Byron Nelson, for example, had practically owned the tour in 1944 and 1945. Hogan had tasted success (he was the tour's leading money winner in 1940, 1941, 1942, and again in 1946), but in 1948 he was nearly untouchable. He won eleven tournaments that year, including the PGA Championship, and led the tour with $32,112 in winnings and a strokes-per-round average of 69.30. Clearly, Hogan was the class act of the tour.

Hogan's U.S. Open record, however, had been mixed. His first appearance was in 1939, the year Nelson won after Snead's costly miscalculation. Hogan finished sixty-second that year. He had won the 1942 exhibition in Chicago, but it wasn't until six years later that Hogan finally broke through. He led an assault on the Riviera Country Club that will long be remembered. Hogan shot the lights out, firing 67 in the opening round, then reeling off rounds of 72, 68, and 69 in succession. It all added up to a stunning 276, obliterating the record of 281 set by Ralph Guldahl in 1937. Hogan's total of eight under par was also a tournament record. This is not to say others played poorly: Jimmy Demaret was only two strokes behind, and in fact, no fewer than five golfers beat par.

As a result, when Hogan, the Vardon Trophy winner, the golfer with the lowest stroke average, won the U.S. Open it was only the second of four times that the tour's finest golfer of the season won the national championship.

1 9 4 9

MEDINAH COUNTRY CLUB
CHICAGO · ILLINOIS

The golf world was still reeling when the professionals gathered at Medinah in early June. Four months earlier, Ben Hogan had been seriously injured in an automobile accident. He was lucky to be alive, much less seriously thinking about defending his U.S. Open title. Though Hogan desperately wanted to play, he couldn't will his battered body to the task. Thus, it was literally an open field, anyone's tournament to win.

With Hogan out, Sam Snead seemed the logical choice. He would finish 1949 and 1950 as the tour's leading money winner and win the Vardon Trophy for best stroke average. Still, he had already thrown away the national title in 1939 and 1947. This time, it was Dr. Cary Middlecoff who played the spoiler's role in Snead's drive for the Open title.

Middlecoff was entering his prime: 1949 was the year he led the professional tour with seven victories. Still, the former dentist had started raggedly, shooting a 75 on his first trip around Medinah's Number Three course. Middlecoff then rallied with a searing 67 in the second round and a 69 in the third, for an aggregate of 211, to take a three-stroke lead over Clayton Heafner. Snead was six strokes back, seemingly out of contention.

Then Middlecoff reverted to first-round form. He ballooned to another 75 in the crucible of the final eighteen holes and his total of 286 looked exceedingly vulnerable. Back on the course, Heafner and Snead began to score. Though Heafner was even through fourteen holes, he finished with a 73 and a four-round score of 287, one shy of Middlecoff. Snead, however, had twice as many shots to make up. He opened the front nine with a credible 36 and, with Middlecoff already in the comfort and safety of the clubhouse, knew a 69 would give him his first U.S. Open. In true Snead fashion, he almost did it. Almost.

Snead's putter came to life and, much to the gallery's pleasure, he caught Middlecoff on the fourteenth hole with a birdie. Par golf the rest of the way would force a playoff; a birdie would win. Snead played conservatively and scored par on the fifteenth and sixteenth, but the deceptively difficult par-three seventeenth was his undoing. Snead, putting from off the fringe, knocked his second shot well past the hole. His putt for par failed and now only a birdie on the final hole could salvage a tie. Snead's long chip for a birdie was short, though, and he lost by a single stroke.

1 9 5 0

MERION GOLF CLUB
ARDMORE · PENNSYLVANIA

Ben Hogan's fabulous 1948 season had blended almost seamlessly into 1949, when he won two of the first four tournaments and finished second in another, losing to Jimmy Demaret in a playoff. Then, on February 2, 1949, a bus traveling on Highway 80 between Fort Worth and Van Horn, Texas, did something that no golfer had been able to do in recent years: it stopped Ben Hogan in his tracks.

The morning fog was thick. Hogan didn't see the headlights of the oncoming bus until it was too late. His athletic reflexes may have saved his life, as well as that of his wife, Valerie. In the split second he realized that a head-on collision was inescapable, Hogan threw himself toward the passenger seat, where Valerie was sitting. He was grazed by the steering wheel as it was driven toward the seat. The front of the car was compressed into the passenger compartment, pinning his left leg. It was ninety minutes before Hogan was pulled from the wreckage and the drive to the El Paso hospital approached an additional two hours. Hogan's legs were badly mutilated, and the string of broken bones (pelvis, shoulder, rib, and ankle) was formidable.

Hogan was made of championship timber, though. He fought, and he fought hard. Two weeks later, Hogan had rallied famously and seemed out of immediate danger when he encountered a serious setback. A blood clot, traveling from Hogan's damaged left leg, moved through his body and settled in his lungs. A hasty operation and a number of blood transfusions saved his life, but Hogan was confined to a hospital for nearly two months. He immediately began a rigorous rehabilitation, for determination had always been his hallmark.

UPI/Bettmann

ABOVE: *Dr. Cary Middlecoff, the Memphis dentist, celebrated poolside with his wife, Edith, after winning the 1949 U.S. Open at Medinah Country Club in Chicago.* OPPOSITE PAGE: *Ben Hogan's breathtaking return to championship form came in 1950 at Merion Golf Club in Ardmore, Pennsylvania. Unable to use golf carts, as they were not permitted in competition, to ease the pain in his throbbing legs, Hogan withstood the challenge of a grueling playoff.*

Hogan, after all, was not merely blessed with his beautifully balanced swing. He developed it, refined it, earned it through thousands and thousands of hours of tedious practice. He did not win his first professional tournament until the age of twenty-five, or his first major title until he was thirty-three. His skill with a club combined with his mental toughness, the resolve that allowed him to stroke bold, confident putts and play his shots always mindful of the next one made an unbeatable combination.

Accordingly, the accident only slowed him down. Most people would have worried about relearning how to walk, but as he recovered at his home in Fort Worth, Hogan convinced himself that he would be able to return to the professional tour. Before 1949 ended, he was driving balls at the nearby Colonial Country Club.

Hogan chose the Los Angeles Open, played at the site of his 1948 U.S. Open triumph, the Riviera Country Club, as his first test. Clearly, Hogan was not completely himself yet. In fact, his legs pained him greatly; excessive walking left them swollen and cramped. Hogan's swing, too, had changed. Before the accident it had been a low, aggressive stroke that was more slash than silk. He usually had been long off the tee, and had paid the price in terms of accuracy. After the crash, however, Hogan's backswing was noticeably shorter. That led to a little less distance as well as fewer adventures in the rough, a subtle change in style that would serve him well on the typically tight and demanding courses of the U.S. Open.

Hogan's endurance was pushed to the limit in the first round at Los Angeles. In practice rounds, Hogan had spared his legs with golf carts, but they weren't permitted in competition.

FPG International

73

AP/Wide World Photos

He opened with a round of 73 that seemed covered with rust, then reeled off three consecutive 69s for a total of 280 that only Sam Snead could match. Hogan lost the playoff by four strokes, prompting him to observe, "I still have a long way to go." Still, his dramatic return left his peers and the public looking ahead to the U.S. Open, to be played at Merion Golf Club. It would mark the national championship's golden anniversary, its fiftieth staging.

In the only major tournament before the June Open, Hogan was in contention at the Masters with a round to go, but faded badly over the last eighteen holes and finished tied for fourth. Hogan's first round at Merion seemed to suggest he was still a year or so away from a complete recovery. He shot a two-over-par 72 (he had stumbled to a start of 39 on the front nine, then followed with a smart 33 on the back nine), a score generally good enough to be in contention. The problem was that someone named Lee Mackey had scorched the fabled course with a 64 and Hogan trailed by eight strokes. Hogan's first-round score, however, had belied a growing confidence. His second-round score of 69 moved him to a total of 141, within striking distance. That was the good news. The bad news? After single rounds on Thursday and Friday, the U.S. Open format called for both closing rounds on Saturday. Hogan, who had played with his legs wrapped in heavy elastic bandages, spent much of Friday night in a tub of hot water, soaking his aching limbs.

Hogan navigated the third round without mishap. He shot a modest 72, leaving him tied with playing partner Cary Middlecoff and two strokes behind leader Lloyd Mangrum, the 1946 champion. Dutch Harrison was one stroke off the pace. With the tension mounting and the course rising to its own defense, Hogan opened with a less-than-scintillating 37 over the first nine holes. Though he didn't know it at the time, Hogan had vaulted into the lead essentially by standing still. Middlecoff and Mangrum were two shots back and Harrison trailed by three. While the front-runners set about the business of winning, George Fazio slipped quietly into the clubhouse with a final aggregate of 287. As the afternoon faded, that score began to loom large. After Mangrum managed to match Fazio's total, all eyes turned to Hogan for an agonizing hour.

He had gamely attacked Merion for more than three rounds but, almost inevitably, Hogan's legs seemed to leave him down the stretch. Ahead by three shots on the twelfth hole, Hogan seriously wondered if he had the stamina to finish. Oddly enough, it was his putter that betrayed him. Hogan had no trouble reaching the twelfth and fifteenth holes, but he used three putts on each green and his lead dwindled to a single stroke with three tough holes yet to play. He lost that shot on the seventeenth; surely, the eighteenth would finish him. Hogan, informed that a par would force a three-way tie with Fazio and Mangrum, chose a safe one-iron to the green and dropped the ball about forty feet from the hole. The swollen gallery roared as Hogan dragged himself up the fairway toward the green. He was limping noticeably now and, when his putt slid four feet past the hole, he wondered if all the pain and suffering was worth it. When his bid for par fell into the cup, Hogan wondered if he could face the eighteen-hole playoff. His mind said yes; his legs, well....

More than anything, Hogan's victory in the 1950 U.S. Open was a triumph of mind and spirit. His real victory was on Saturday, when he carried himself through those thirty-six holes with extraordinary determination. The playoff was almost anticlimac-

tic. Fazio self-destructed early and finished with a 75. Mangrum drew a two-stroke penalty on the sixteenth hole for cleaning his ball on the green and scored a 73. Hogan, who sank a fifty-foot birdie putt on the seventeenth hole, produced a truly golden 69. Ben Hogan was again the best golfer in the game. He would win sixty-three professional tournaments in his career, third only to Sam Snead and Jack Nicklaus, but he always maintained that the 1950 U.S. Open meant the most to him.

1 9 5 1

OAKLAND HILLS COUNTRY CLUB
BIRMINGHAM · MICHIGAN

What would Ben Hogan do for an encore? He had already authored one of the great comebacks in golfing history—in sports history, for that matter. He still wasn't playing full-time on the professional tour, but had, as always, picked his spots with care. Earlier that spring, Hogan had won the Masters tournament, a title that somehow had previously eluded him. Thus, he came into the U.S. Open at Oakland Hills as the favorite, an unhappy favorite at that.

As long as the USGA lays out courses, players will complain that the courses are unfair. When Hogan suggested that the fairways in the revamped course were too tight, however, it sounded like a reasonable criticism. The golfers, afraid to make a mistake, declined to attack the course and were consumed in the process.

Bobby Locke survived the first two rounds better than anyone, posting a modest 144. Hogan, who had been strangely docile with his drives, produced a 76 and a 73, placing him a staggering nine strokes over par and five shots behind Locke. His third-round 71 was a little more aggressive, but he still trailed Locke and Jimmy Demaret by two strokes. Hogan and Clayton Heafner, who had tied Snead for second in the 1949

OPPOSITE PAGE: *In 1953, Ben Hogan became the third man in the history of the Open to win four trophies. On the whole, however, his 1953 season, during which he won five out of six 72-hole events, may have been the greatest ever played.*

In 1952, an anonymous thirty-two-year-old professional named Julius Boros beat the heat in Dallas and took home the U.S. Open title. Here, Boros chips to the eighth green.

AP/Wide World Photos

U.S. Open, were tied at 220, an even ten strokes past par. Who would emerge in the afternoon's final round?

In his mind, Hogan had finally figured out how to beat Oakland Hills. It took him another nine holes to produce any results, but when the fire in him began to burn, he started aiming directly at the delicately placed flagsticks. He shot a seemingly routine 35 on the front nine, level par, and had been in position to do better. On the back nine, however, Hogan opened with a birdie on the testing tenth hole. A monstrous drive, a laser of a two-iron, and a confident four-foot putt signaled that Hogan meant business. Then he birdied the fifteenth. As Locke and Demaret slipped back, Hogan charged on. He birdied the eighteenth hole to complete a 67, the best round of the tournament. Heafner himself shot a 69 to finish second, two strokes back. Hogan had gone around the back nine in a sizzling 32 and later would claim that the closing round at Oakland Hills was the best of his career. Certainly, it was the second-lowest by an Open winner, but Sarazen's 66 in 1923 had come on the far easier Fresh Meadow course.

Hogan, never one to mince words, said, "I'm glad I brought this course, this monster, to its knees." And when he said that, it didn't sound like bragging.

1 9 5 2

NORTHWOOD CLUB
DALLAS · TEXAS

Ben Hogan had now won three U.S. Opens, a feat surpassed only by Willie Anderson, who had won in 1901, 1903, 1904, and 1905, and Bobby Jones. Considering his recent championship record and the fact that this U.S. Open was being staged in his home state of Texas, Hogan was an overwhelming favorite. Over the first two rounds, Hogan looked as good as his press clippings—maybe even better.

But while Hogan was shooting matching 69s, Julius Boros very quietly crept into contention with a pair of 71s. Most people were watching Hogan and his two closest pursuers, George Fazio, 140, and Johnny Bulla, 141, when Boros made his move in the third round on Saturday.

Boros had been in contention on the final day at Oakland Hills, so he was hardly anonymous when his name began soaring on the leaderboard. Still, at thirty-two years old, Boros was not a typical touring professional. He had come to the game of golf late and he had a nonchalant swing and a seemingly carefree attitude as he worked from tee to green. Under the brutal Texas sun, Boros calmly shot a blistering 68. It was a round that put him well over the top. Boros' three-round total of 210 was the tournament's best, and when he came back in the afternoon with a 71, it was all over. Fazio and Bulla never challenged and Ed Oliver climbed through the wreckage to finish second.

Hogan's final day was curiously devoid of intensity. He shot identical scores of 74 to finish third. Perhaps, as some said, the heat got the best of Hogan, who would turn forty later that year. Maybe it was just a signal that he was mortal. Then again, maybe not.

1 9 5 3

OAKMONT COUNTRY CLUB
OAKMONT · PENNSYLVANIA

Rumors of Ben Hogan's demise dogged him after the failure at Northwood. He was getting on in years and no one could stay at the top forever. Hogan himself knew that he had underachieved in 1952 and maniacally worked on his game during the off-season. He came out smoking and won the Masters tournament, which had gradually become recognized as one of the four major championships. Hogan set a new aggregate record at Augusta and continued to tear up the professional tour in the weeks leading to the U.S. Open at Oakmont.

Just as he had in the final round at Oakland Hills two years earlier, Hogan dismantled the course. He fired a five-under-par 67, which was three strokes better than the rest of the field. Pursued by Sam Snead, Hogan put together three consistent rounds of 72, 73, and 71 to capture his fourth U.S. Open in six years. (Hogan's score of 283 was an incredible sixteen shots better than the total Sam Parks, Jr., had posted at the 1935 Open at Oakmont.) Snead, who had trailed by only one stroke seven holes from the finish, collapsed in typical U.S. Open fashion by giving up five strokes down the stretch to finish six shots back. It was Snead's fourth second-place finish.

Though Oakmont would see the last of his U.S. Open mastery, Ben Hogan was really just beginning an amazing year. Bobby Jones had been a golf legend for several years now; with this triumph Hogan had matched Jones' four Open titles —and had done it in two fewer years. More tantalizing still, Hogan seemed to be in a position to challenge what most experts considered the game's finest season, Jones' Grand Slam of 1930. In Jones' day, the U.S. Open, the British Open, and the amateur championships of both nations were considered the four major tournaments. As professional golf took hold, however, the Masters and the PGA championship supplanted the two amateur tournaments in most people's minds.

If circumstances hadn't prevented it, Hogan might have made the sweep; the thing that prevented him from entering both championships was a scheduling conflict. In a quirk of timing, Hogan would have been required to appear on both sides of the Atlantic on the same day to manage the feat. The day of the final PGA match, July 7, was also the second day of qualifying for the British Open. Hogan had decided some time earlier that he would try to follow in the footsteps of U.S. golfers like Jones, Walter Hagen, and Gene Sarazen by winning the British Open. He had never played in Britain before, but Hogan's analytical mind quickly sized up the classic links course at Carnoustie, Scotland. His game grew sharper with each round. His scores, 73, 71, 70, and 68, were good enough to produce a four-stroke victory.

Hogan returned to the United States a conquering hero. Like Jones, he was feted with a ticker tape parade in New York. And why not? All told, Hogan entered six seventy-two-hole tournaments and won five of them. No golfer would threaten Jones' single season of success to the extent that Hogan did in 1953.

1 9 5 4

BALTUSROL GOLF CLUB
SPRINGFIELD · NEW JERSEY

As the field gathered at Baltusrol in 1954, no one was confusing Ed Furgol with Ben Hogan. Furgol was an anonymous tour professional whose chief distinction was a withered left arm. That was before his heroics on the seventy-second hole. Today, golf historians fondly remember Furgol as a U.S. Open champion.

The original Baltusrol club had been in existence since 1895. After hosting the national championship in 1903 and again in 1915, the layout was torn up and turned into two courses by golf architect A. W. Tillinghast. Tony Manero had won the 1936 Open on the Upper Course; eighteen years later the championship was contested on the Lower Course. To ensure a demanding circuit, Robert Trent Jones had touched up the Lower Course. Furgol, however, found it to his liking. He led Hogan by only one stroke at the midway point, but the legend fell out of the tournament with a 76 in the third round.

It came down to the final hole. Furgol, aware that a par-five on the eighteenth would bring him the championship, promptly hooked his tee shot into the thick trees running along the left side of the hole. The conventional shot would have been a little pitch back into the fairway, but that would have left Furgol too far from the hole. There was another avenue available, though. The finishing holes of the Upper and Lower courses lie next to each other, in full view of the elegant clubhouse. Furgol had a clear path to the fairway of the Upper Course and, after confirming that it was legal, played his shot through the trees to the Upper Course. He pitched back onto the Lower Course green and made the par that gave him a total of 284, one stroke better than newcomer Gene Littler's score.

ABOVE: *Ed Furgol, who crippled his left arm in a playground accident at the age of twelve, made an unlikely, but very happy, Open champion in 1954.* OPPOSITE PAGE: *The members of the gallery crane their necks as Ben Hogan tees off from the thirty-sixth hole during the 1953 Open.*

1 9 5 5

OLYMPIC CLUB
SAN FRANCISCO · CALIFORNIA

In the 1955 Open, the Arctic overcame the Antarctic. An abstract image, maybe, but one that neatly captures the essence of the event. Jack Fleck and Ben Hogan were, after all, the polar opposites of professional golf. Hogan's name figuratively means "champion," while Fleck's means "nebulous matter."

Fleck was an insignificant flea among show dogs until 1955, the year he beat Ben Hogan, golf deity. He and the puckish golf fates thought otherwise, but Fleck had no realistic chance of upsetting Hogan, who was hypnotically stalking his fifth Open title and golf history. The odds grew substantially longer in the first round, when Fleck shot 76, six strokes more than par, four strokes more than Hogan, and nine behind the leader, Tommy "Thunder" Bolt.

Bolt was usually a testy, cranky, cross golfer, who flung almost as many clubs as he swung. In the opening round of the 1955 Open, however, Bolt placidly putted as though he were rolling the confounded ball into an open manhole; he needed only one putt on 11 greens and just 25 overall. Then he lost his putting touch and most of his lead in the second round, during which he shot 77, enabling Hogan and Fleck, each of whom were in second at 145, to catch up.

Hogan, forty-three years old at the time, shot another 72 in the third round and led at the end of fifty-four holes. Sam Snead, the Eternal Contender, was in second at 218, one shot behind Hogan, one shot ahead of Bolt, and two shots in front of Fleck.

The fourth round of the Open is an endurance test, an emotional and psychological battle between the apprehensive golfer and the true enemy, the golf course. The final eighteen holes of the Open typically favor resolute champions with the fierce, almost primal, instinct for winning. Of course, the Open sometimes rewards fortunate survivors, but luck usually trails people with talent, resolve, and initiative—people like Ben Hogan.

Luck sure did appear to be following Hogan around the Olympic Club: he went out in 35, came in identically, and then confidently gave his golf ball to Joe Dey of the USGA as a sou-venir for Golf House, the USGA's headquarters and museum. What was left to do except award Hogan the trophy?

While people were congratulating Hogan on his record achievement, Fleck, the invisible enemy, was shooting 33 on the front nine and secretly creeping into contention on his belly. He strung pars on the first four holes of the incoming nine, but misjudged his approach shot to the fourteenth green and bogeyed there, leaving him two shots behind with four holes remaining. The fickle gallery forsook him until he made up one of the shots at the fifteenth hole with a birdie from eight feet. Pars at sixteen and seventeen did not help him. The stray had one more chance to lasso the cowpoke from Texas, defy probability, and alter history.

Hogan sat in the locker room anxiously answering questions and occasionally observing the unfolding show below from his balcony seat. The scorching klieg lights suddenly shone on Fleck as he acted out the fantasy of every golfer, whether of average or legendary ability.

The eighteenth hole at the Olympic Club, a par-four, did not look menacing on the scorecard; it measured just 337 yards. Short holes often stretch like some predatory viper in the eyes of the golfer needing three to share the lead in the Open. Fleck struck his tee shot in one of those wild, flaming parabolas spectators are apt to see at public driving ranges, the type of inexact shot ordinary golfers in stalls smite weakly toward distant yardage markers. The ball came down in the short rough, about 130 yards from the green. The most important shot and decision of his career were facing Fleck. Before addressing the ball, he had to address this difficult question: what club should he use from such a problematic lie?

He jerked a seven-iron from his bag and launched the ball toward the cup. It arced like an emergency flare in the dress-gray sky, dropped softly onto the green, and stopped less than ten feet to the right of the cup.

Open champions need to be gallant putters, because Open putting surfaces are typically slicker than luge chutes. Golfers with the nerve and ability to perfectly judge the speed and line of critical putts at the Open are rarer than double eagles. As it was, the meter was running on Fleck's surprising ride in the Open. He had one putt to tie Hogan, one putt to inscribe his unknown name in the annals of golf history.

Jack Fleck did the impossible in 1955: he beat the odds and Ben Hogan in overtime at the Olympic Club in San Francisco, California.

UPI/Bettmann

With the unusual composure success in the Open requires, Fleck took the shot of his life and the ball rolled down the slope and into both the cup and history. Anonymous Jack Fleck had shot 67 and 287 overall, tying the magnificent Ben Hogan.

America would have understood if Fleck had immediately withdrawn from the playoff, told Hogan, "Look, I'd love to play tomorrow, but, you know, the plumber is coming…and I made the appointment weeks ago…and you know how difficult it would be to reschedule. So, I'll catch you in 1956, OK?"

Any good excuse would have given Fleck the opportunity to escape, save face, and spare himself likely public humiliation. The world certainly thought Fleck was going to be chloroformed, impaled on pins in a petri dish, and spread out like an insect for dissection. Instead, Fleck played. In overtime, Hogan proved to be human, making bogeys at the fourteenth and seventeenth holes. Fleck had actually outshot Hogan, 69 to 72.

Improbably, Fleck left the Olympic Club with the handsome trophy and the fattest paycheck; Hogan left disconsolately, to say the least.

1 9 5 6

OAK HILL COUNTRY CLUB
ROCHESTER · NEW YORK

Sometimes it takes a person both intimate with and indifferent to pain to challenge and conquer golf, a game that produces much more discomfort than it relieves. It takes someone like a dentist—someone like Cary Middlecoff. Drilling teeth did not stimulate Middlecoff as much as drilling golf balls up and down fairways across the United States. So, in 1947, Middlecoff, the son of a dentist, a graduate of the University of Tennessee Dental College, and an excellent amateur golfer, began playing for a living on the PGA Tour.

He won the Open in 1949 at Medinah Country Club, joining the long roster of golfers who frustrated Sam Snead at the one major tournament that wriggled from his strong grip. Then, in 1956 at Oak Hill Country Club, Middlecoff disappointed Ben Hogan, preventing Hogan from winning his fifth

AP/Wide World Photos

Open. Middlecoff was a skittish competitor during his career—an exposed electrical wire, so to speak. Under pressure, however, he certainly knew how to control the driver and use the putter, two meaningful and usually fickle golfing tools.

He arrived at Oak Hill and calmly shot 71 in the first round and 70 in the second, in spite of two sevens. With thirty-six holes remaining, he trailed Hogan by one stroke and the leader, Peter Thomson, by two. The lead became his with another 70 in the third round. He went around in 35–35 in the fourth round and left the seventy-second hole in first, but was unable to relax or celebrate because Hogan, Julius Boros, and Ted Kroll were tailing him.

One by one Hogan, Boros, and Kroll each blew his chance. Hesitant putting at the sixteenth and eighteenth holes did Hogan in; he had become a man so stricken by nerves that each putt was an indecisive jab, more prayer than stroke. Boros, needing to make just one to tie Middlecoff, lined up birdie putts on three of the last four holes but could not sink one of them, though he came close all three times. Kroll would have won the title with pars on the last four holes, but he bogeyed at the fifteenth hole, and double bogeyed at the sixteenth and seventeenth. He finished with a score of 285, tied with Thomson and Ed Furgol for fourth place.

An elite force of marksmen had shot at Middlecoff from close range, but he ducked and survived, scoring 281 to defeat Hogan and Boros, tied for second at 282.

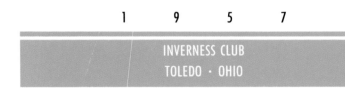

INVERNESS CLUB
TOLEDO · OHIO

In 1957, Cary Middlecoff came to Inverness to golf and hunt. Willie Anderson, Bobby Jones, Ben Hogan, and another Open title were the quarry. Bagging another Open would elevate Middlecoff to the level of Anderson, Jones, and Hogan and make him one of four golfers in history to win at least three Open championships. It would also put him within range of the victory record of four that Anderson, Jones, and Hogan share nowadays with Jack Nicklaus.

One by one some of the best golfers on Earth shot at Dr. Cary Middlecoff (OPPOSITE PAGE) during the 1956 Open, but he wound up surviving the barrage. Middlecoff (ABOVE) won the 1956 Open at Oak Hill Country Club in Rochester, New York.

UPI/Bettmann

He was the favorite because of his status as defending champion and because Hogan had withdrawn from the tournament with pleurisy, a respiratory ailment. But halfway through the tournament Dick Mayer and Billy Joe Patton led at 138, matching the tournament record at the time. Middlecoff was eight shots behind, following rounds of 71 and 75.

Overtaking Patton was easy—Patton shot successive 76s in the third and fourth rounds. Mayer and a sentimental contender from another generation, Jimmy Demaret, were now Middlecoff's obstructions.

Demaret's closet was full of gaudy souvenirs from the Masters. He wore the garish green jacket in 1940, 1947, and 1950; the Open, however, had always eluded him. He did not figure to challenge for the title at the age of forty-seven, since golfing relics rarely contend at major championships. Nonetheless, he entered the clubhouse Saturday afternoon with an aggregate of 283 and a lot of hope. Mayer shot 74 in the third round and came to the eighteenth hole needing a four to tie Demaret and a three to eliminate him.

The last hole at Inverness is a runt, unless you need a birdie there to win the Open—then it extends to the next galaxy. The hole is arithmetically inconsequential, measuring only 330 yards from tee box to green. Do not let its shrunken dimensions deceive you. The hole may be short, but it is merciless.

Diabolical Donald Ross, Inverness' designer, laid several traps in front of and to the left of the small green to snare imprecise shots. To remain in first place, Mayer had to reach the putting surface without springing one of the traps. He struck his tee shot perfectly in the center of the fairway, then pitched his ball beyond the front traps and the cup. Golf balls go forward and in reverse but only masters know how to regularly engage the second gear; Mayer was just such an expert. The ball spun backward and stopped a mere eight feet from the cup. Mayer sank the putt and broke Demaret's heart. "The boy made a wonderful, wonderful putt," Demaret said politely, sincerely, dejectedly.

The tournament did not end at the seventy-second hole. Middlecoff shot 68 in the morning round and was charging at Mayer from behind. Another 68 in the afternoon round and he would catch the leader, but he was at even par with four holes remaining.

Dick Mayer (OPPOSITE PAGE) *beat the heat and Dr. Cary Middlecoff at the 1957 Open. Truculent Tommy Bolt* (RIGHT) *kept calm and cool, and collected the winner's check at the end of the 1958 Open.*

Par at the fifteenth hole meant he somehow had to make threes at two of the last three holes, all par-fours. He made one of the birdies at the sixteenth hole from twenty feet. Par at the seventeenth provided Middlecoff with one more opportunity to tie Mayer. He reached the eighteenth green in regulation; he would leave the hole sharing first place with Mayer or second place with Demaret.

Middlecoff's birdie putt from ten feet initially drifted far to the right, as if it were a car being steered by a drowsy driver. Then, as if its driver awoke just in time to correct its wayward course, the ball slowed down, swerved toward the hole, and parked at the bottom of the cup.

In the playoff, about the only thing that was hot was the temperature, which approached 100 degrees Farenheit. Middlecoff's game and nerves dissolved in the heat. He shot 79 and lost by seven strokes to Mayer, who somehow did not vaporize in the furnace conditions.

1 9 5 8

SOUTHERN HILLS COUNTRY CLUB
TULSA · OKLAHOMA

In 1958 the old order of golf began unraveling like a worn grip. The most conspicuous sign of change was that Sam Snead, who heretofore had been able to duck the twin punches of age and the cut, did not qualify for the final thirty-six holes of the Open for the first time in eighteen years. The most notable sign of change was that Gary Player, one of "The Triumvirate of Golf" in the 1960s (with Arnold Palmer and Jack Nicklaus), wound up finishing second in his first Open.

Truculent Tommy Bolt, a human hurricane, won the title. In his prime years Bolt was as unpredictable and ferocious as Scottish weather patterns. His motto and mantra was, "If you are going to throw a club, it is important to throw it ahead of you,

so you don't waste energy going back to pick it up." (He is infamous for having thrown his driver into a lake at Cherry Hills Country Club in Denver during the 1960 U.S. Open.)

In 1958 Bolt controlled his combustible temper and managed his estimable game all four rounds. He shot 71, 71, 69, and 72 for an aggregate of 283 at troublesome Southern Hills; he led from starting line to finish line, and won the tournament by four strokes over Player, his emotional opposite. Player, who still competes and contends on the PGA Senior Tour, walks purposefully up fairways, looking as though he is heading somewhere farther, indeed somewhere other, than just the next green.

Player, twenty-two years old at the time, did not begin playing golf until he was fifteen, but his dedication to fitness and the game has made him one of the most prolific golfers of all time.

1 9 5 9

WINGED FOOT GOLF CLUB
MAMARONECK · NEW YORK

The Winged Foot Golf Club course was created following the deliberately devious design of master architect A. W. Tillinghast, who was commissioned to build a man-size course. Tom Nieporte, now the club pro, remembers his introduction, or more precisely, his indoctrination to Winged Foot. It was thirty days prior to the 1959 U.S. Open, and Nieporte industriously read newspaper stories about the merciless course. The contents, exaggerated some here, were alarming: rough so tall golfers would require scythes to hack back onto the fairway; rough so tall golfers would require bloodhounds to locate their golf balls in the thick green stuff; rough so tall golfers would probably lose their golf balls, golf bags, and sanity in the wicked weeds.

There were also the stupefying details of holes fifteen through eighteen, a series of oppressively difficult par-fours that the members had christened Death Valley years ago. "The stories were intimidating," Nieporte says. "By the time you arrived, you were afraid to play the course."

Winged Foot did not look so fearsome when Billy Casper left the seventy-second hole. Casper won the 1959 Open with his touch of velvet on the greens. He struck the ball 282 times in all, but merely 114 times with his supernatural putter in four rounds.

The faces of professional golf were changing weekly, as were the winning scores and tournament sites. Casper's potbelly probably stuck out more than his face when he won his first Open. Casper, then twenty-seven years old then, was quietly turning into one of the heavyweights of the game, as much for his remarkable putting ability as for his prodigious proportions.

The tournament began on faraway fairways, with Ben Hogan temporarily reverting to old form. Hogan shot 32 on the tricky front nine but 37 on the incoming nine and had to share the lead with Dick Knight and two future Open champions, slender Gene Littler and resolute Gary Player.

Casper, two shots behind at the first tee, waved his magical putter 31 times in the second round and presto! He led at 139. He shot 69 in the third round, swelling his lead to three strokes over Hogan at the end of fifty-four holes. The Big Greenskeeper in the Sky watered the course in the afternoon, submerging some of the fairways and greens and converting the golf club into a yacht basin.

Thirsty cornstalks in Iowa would have welcomed all the rain that fell on Mamaroneck Saturday afternoon; some areas of the course had the consistency of saturated carpeting, causing USGA officials to postpone the fourth round until Sunday, marking the first time the Open was held over four days.

Casper did not finish like a champion, but he did win. He shot a 74 on a gusty, lead-gray afternoon. Hogan had another opportunity to capture his fifth Open, but went around in 76 and instead wound up in tenth place.

Casper barely won the last Open of the 1950s, edging Mike Souchak and Bob Rosburg by one shot and more accurately by one club's length—that of his sensational putter. Golf was about to enter the 1960s, the television age, and take off like a Mercury rocket.

Billy Casper won the last open of the 1950s with his magnificent putting on the treacherous greens at Winged Foot Golf Club in Mamaroneck, New York.

1 9 6 0

CHERRY HILLS COUNTRY CLUB
DENVER · COLORADO

Informality and vitality—Arnold Palmer gave both to golf in 1960. He did not invent the game, although it seems he deserves almost as much credit as the ancient Scots for its origination. What Palmer did do was perfect professional golf, transforming a small business into a nationwide corporate enterprise by hitching up his pants and being himself: courageous, fearless, and telegenic.

He gave professional golf personality and, furthermore, television appeal. Professional golfers earn corporate executive

UPI/Bettmann

wages these days because Palmer made golf entertaining and popular outside the portcullises of private country clubs. His charisma gave golf more than galleries; his charisma gave golf a worldwide audience.

Finishing second, fifth, eighth, or any of the careful positions on the leaderboard, did not interest Palmer when he was younger. Placing first was always his objective. Absolute proof of his purpose is visible at the first tee of Cherry Hills Country Club. A plaque there commemorates one of the most astonishing and memorable tee shots in golf history, Palmer's first shot in the final round of the 1960 U.S. Open.

When that round began, Palmer trailed fourteen golfers. He was seven shots behind the leader, Mike Souchak. At lunch in between the third and fourth rounds, Arnie, two miles behind in a one-mile race, thought he had enough time to catch Souchak. Of course, Souchak's survival was the main topic among the golfers gathering in the grill. Palmer ate, speculated, and calculated his odds of winning the Open with Ken Venturi, Bob Rosburg, and golf writer Bob Drum.

"I may shoot 65," Palmer said. "What would you do?"

"Nothing," Drum growled. "You're too far back."

The remark was the flint and fuse that detonated Palmer, who has even more confidence than money—and he earns millions of dollars annually from golf and business interests.

"The hell I am," he told Drum. "A 65 would give me 280, and 280 wins Opens."

Retreat was an unpardonable option, he thought. Attack the field and the course, that was his adventurous strategy. The beachhead was the first hole, 346 yards from tee to flag.

Placement was thought to be more important than power there. Palmer, though, unsheathed his driver, his weapon of choice on the first hole in the previous three rounds, when he had made six, five, and four, respectively. Special golfers like Palmer expect to make three on such short holes. In this instance, though, he was thinking eagle, not birdie. He drew back his driver and in no time the speeding clubhead struck the face of the stationary golf ball squarely, with the identical impact the business end of a baseball bat produces against an incoming fastball. *Whack!*

When he swings, Palmer exhibits the countenance of childbirth: so much grimacing, so much tension, so much release,

APWide World Photos

Arnold Palmer (OPPOSITE PAGE) boldly won the 1960 Open at Cherry Hills Country Club in Denver. Primarily with impetus from the most famous tee shot in golf history, Arnold Palmer (LEFT) recruited members of his Army while stampeding to victory at the 1960 Open, a seminal golf tournament.

so much rapture, all simultaneously. He does not rhythmically sweep a golf ball from the tee or ground. He slashes violently at the ball with the same chopping motion lumberjacks use to fell an old tree with an axe.

The force he created with his swing was powerful enough to launch his golf ball 340 yards, and inaugurate an entire era. The nature of the tournament and of professional golf, for that matter, changed with one remarkable drive. In the crucible of the sport, the tee box, where more golfers melt than deliver, Palmer forged the most famous drive of all time. His face never displayed so much as a tic of anxiety; his swing was not the spasmed, short-armed jerk of an apprehensive golfer. "It was

the 'sweetness' of the risk that I remember, and not its dangers," he wrote of the experience in his autobiography.

Palmer did not sink the eagle putt, but three was an acceptable score, because the birdie triggered one of the most explosive stretches of golf in history. He chipped in for birdie at the second hole, and made another birdie at the third. He birdied at the fourth by sinking a snaking forty-foot putt. A par-five at the fifth hole interrupted the birdie binge, but Palmer made up more ground with birdies at the sixth and seventh holes. Palmer and Souchak were tied by the tenth hole. Palmer was ahead by the twelfth hole. He went out in 30 and was furious he did not shoot 29.

AP/Wide World Photos

In all, Palmer overtook the fourteen golfers ahead of him and crushed the hopes of another dozen contenders, including Ben Hogan and the runner-up, amateur Jack Nicklaus, who was only twenty years old at the time.

Palmer did shoot 65 in the final round, for an aggregate of 280 for the championship. His boldness and determination made the difference in that seminal golf tournament. But then, daring defines his career and life and distinguishes both from those of other exceptional golfers.

1 9 6 1

OAKLAND HILLS COUNTRY CLUB
BIRMINGHAM · MICHIGAN

Golf, the most maddening diversion of all time, always feigns vulnerability before bushwacking its suckered prey. Golf shamelessly deludes its victims, falsely empowers and emboldens them, then ferociously counterattacks. Arnold Palmer frequently won battles against Golf, but Golf always wins in the end. Always.

In 1961 General Palmer and his Army came to Oakland Hills Country Club to behead "The Monster," to conquer another Open. Instead, one of the foot soldiers, Gene Littler, slew the ferocious adversary. In fact, Palmer did not even engage the enemy. He shot four ineffective rounds at Oakland Hills from close range and did nothing more than survive the cut.

Littler won the sole major tournament of his professional career, shooting rounds of 73, 68, 72, 68 for an aggregate score of 281. Par beat him by one shot, which was also his margin of victory against colorless Bob Goalby and kaleidoscopic Doug Sanders (whose lavender and yellow golf wardrobe was conspicuous among the racks and racks of Wonder Bread– white shirts and navy blue trousers, the conformist work clothes of most golfers at the time).

The Amateur champion more than thirty years before, Littler embodied the confounding nature of this popular and perplexing sport. He swung clubs with the same elegance and authority as Sam Snead and Ben Hogan for three decades and remains one of the demigods of Golf.

AP/Wide World Photos

Gene Littler (ABOVE AND OPPOSITE PAGE) *remains one of the mystery men of golf. He swung as sweetly as Sam Snead and Ben Hogan, but his skimpy major tournament portfolio did not contain much besides the 1961 Open title.*

Jack Nicklaus began his collection of major tournament titles, eighteen and counting, at the 1972 Open by defeating Arnold Palmer in what would be one of their many jousts.

AP/Wide World Photos

1 9 6 2

OAKMONT COUNTRY CLUB
OAKMONT · PENNSYLVANIA

Some sports rivalries resemble the first salvo at Fourth of July fireworks displays: spectacular explosions that last several seconds, then fizzle and vanish. The initial bursts interest us, but we leave remembering the Grand Finale. In the 1960s the golf equivalent of thrilling pyrotechnics was Jack Nicklaus versus Arnold Palmer, or Fat Jack versus Audacious Arnie.

Nicklaus and Palmer were the headliners, the main act, of professional golf. Their presence at tournaments attracted galleries ranging from rambunctious fight crowds to peaceful country club gatherings. "Go get 'em, Arnie" and "Get tough, Arnie" were the battle cries of Palmer's enthusiastic Army. Nicklaus, in his twenties at the time, repeatedly was the target of the churlish enlistees' needling. Watching the skillful prince challenge and overthrow their king initially upset the intolerant subjects.

Oakmont Country Club was the site of their first significant joust. Palmer had won the British Open the previous July and the Masters in April, so his worshipful homegrown rooters were hoping to see him add another U.S. Open title to his mantel of major championships.

Gene Littler, the defending champion, went around in 69 and led at the end of the first round. Palmer, two shots behind Littler, was one shot ahead of Nicklaus, who had gone on a birdie binge from the first through third holes. Palmer had begun par, bogey, bogey, but had then strung five threes on the back nine, three of them birdies.

Palmer, with 68, and Bob Rosburg, with 69, caught and overtook Littler in the second round. Nicklaus, a golf prodigy in the tradition of Bobby Jones, shot 70. Palmer drove the green and sank an eagle putt from about fifteen feet at the seventeenth hole to lead through fifty-four holes, but had company in first place. He and Bobby Nichols were at 212, one under par. A bogey at the eighteenth hole cost Palmer one precious shot and the outright lead. Nicklaus overshot par by one stroke, but his 72 put him within two shots of Palmer, the favorite-son candidate to win the Open.

When the fourth round began, the crowd had grown in proportion to the drama. In all there were more than 21,000 spectators on the grounds, most of them recruits in Arnie's Army. In order to win now, Nicklaus, in his first season of professional golf, would have to singlehandedly oppose the course, Palmer, and all those rowdy reinforcements. Uncommon concentration and determination differentiate Nicklaus from other special golfers, enabling him to overcome such distractions and avoid misfortune.

Neither a bogey on the first hole nor the partisan cheering of Palmer supporters sabotaged him. He shot 69 in the final round and 283 overall. Nicklaus left the last green in first place, but could not engrave his name on the Open trophy immediately because Palmer still had some opportunities to seize the prize and the moment from him.

Birdies at the second and fourth holes had put Palmer two under for the round and three under for fifty-eight holes. In an attempt to win the title at the sixty-third hole, Palmer decided to test his courage and the benevolence of the golfing gods at the ninth hole, a par-five.

He struck his tee shot accurately and powerfully. In his mind Palmer had to answer one question before reaching his ball: bold eagle or safe birdie? Since he did not build his fortune and reputation on a flimsy foundation of caution, Palmer unsheathed his three-wood and lunged at the ball with all his strength and resolve. The cut shot, though struck solidly, drifted into the right rough and rested on grass flattened by the gallery. In no position to make an eagle, Palmer was merely a good chip and putt from a birdie, perhaps the winning number. Instead he stubbed his third shot, chipped weakly to eight feet, then missed a par putt, and unexpectedly left the green scrawling an infuriating six on his scorecard.

He has spent his entire golf career straddling the divide separating reckless from fearless. That shot at the ninth hole fell onto the heap of gambles he lost, a pile about level with the stack of wagers that Palmer has won.

Turning birdie into bogey at the ninth hole almost extinguished him; Palmer went around the course emitting low-flame intensity from there. All his lead, once four shots, was gone with five holes remaining in regulation. Palmer squandered chances to close out Nicklaus at the seventeenth and eighteenth holes. Each time, birdie putts slid past the hole on greens slicker than wet pavement. He shot 73 in the morning round and 71 in the afternoon and wound up sharing first place with Nicklaus.

The following afternoon Nicklaus began his record collection of professional major championships, now eighteen and counting, by defeating Palmer 71 to 74, in a playoff that had less pop than a firecracker with a wet fuse.

1 9 6 3

THE COUNTRY CLUB
BROOKLINE · MASSACHUSETTS

Perhaps the spirits in charge mistook the 1963 Open trophy for a solid gold pocket watch (the traditional reward for longevity and meritorious service). How else is one to explain Julius Boros' victory at the age of forty-three, which was the retirement age for most golfers back then?

Although Boros had shot an admirable 72, the lowest score of the fourth round, he did not expect to be the recipient of the big prize. In fact, he was in the clubhouse emptying his locker, certain that his aggregate score of 293, nine strokes over par, would be far too high to take first place—293 was the magic number, as it turned out.

Arnold Palmer, the King of Swing and the perpetual Open favorite in the 1960s, sank an insidious par putt from five feet behind the seventy-second hole, tying Boros' score. Texan Jacky Cupit looked like he would be the champion until he left the seventy-first green branding an ugly double bogey on his scorecard. The six at this par-four hole left him sharing the lead with Boros and Palmer. Cupit would have won the 1963 Open with a birdie on the final hole, but his birdie putt from twelve feet slid past the low side of the cup.

The score of 293 that was shared by Boros, Cupit, and Palmer in 1963 was the highest leading score after 72 holes in U.S. Open competition since 1935. (Sam Parks won the 1935 Open with the uncharacteristically high score of 299.) Normally, 293 would have paid middle-of-the-road money, but the weather, especially the wind, inflated the scores. New England

was as windy and chilly as Scotland itself; as a result, even the great golfers' games were as unpredictable as Scottish weather patterns.

In the fourth round only three golfers shot 72 or better—nearly five times that many shot 80 or more, and Tommy Aaron shot 91, the type of ugly score on an Open course that would never satisfy the player who swings his club to meet mortgage payments.

The tournament went into overtime at The Country Club, just as it had fifty years earlier when Francis Ouimet, an American amateur, launched the U.S. Open by singlehandedly vanquishing the British tag team of Harry Vardon and Ted Ray. The 1963 playoff, however, was less dramatic. Boros shot 33 on the front nine and led the field by three shots.

Trailing by four shots after bogeying the tenth hole, Palmer jutted his jaw, coiled his muscles, and set out to attack the course with his mighty swing, the weapon with which he had won the 1960 Open at the Cherry Hills Country Club. This time, however, he hooked his tee ball into a thicket of trees, where it lodged itself in a rotting tree stump. In an attempt to avoid a two-stroke penalty, the aggressive Palmer chose to play the ball as it lay. He chopped at the stump with an iron club and finally dislodged the ball, walking away from the par-four scratching a seven on his scorecard. Although he birdied three of his last four holes, Arnold finished third with a 76, three strokes behind Cupit and six behind Boros.

Boros, with his sweet tempo, imperturbable nature, and silk-on-silk swing, shot an effortless 70 and left Brookline, Massachusetts, with a companion for the Open trophy he had taken home in 1952.

AP/Wide World Photos

*Though all eyes were on Jack
Nicklaus as he putted on the last
hole at The Country Club in 1963
(OPPOSITE PAGE), the real star was Julius
Boros (LEFT). At forty-three, an age
when most professional golfers of
the time were belting golf balls at
some retirement resort, Boros
won the U.S. Open.*

RIGHT: *Ken Venturi receives the rewards of victory at the 1964 Open: the handsome trophy and an affectionate nuzzle from his wife.*
OPPOSITE PAGE: *Venturi snaps his fingers as he comes in five under par on the first nine holes of the final round of the 1964 Open.*

AP/Wide World Photos

1 9 6 4

CONGRESSIONAL COUNTRY CLUB
WASHINGTON · DISTRICT OF COLUMBIA

Sometimes at golf tournaments we learn more about the contestants than their names, hometowns, and country club affiliations. Ken Venturi once let the world gaze at his soul through his soaked shirt. Venturi gallantly won the 1964 U.S. Open at Congressional Country Club during a week of hell. In sweltering conditions hot enough to thaw even the glacial Ben Hogan, Venturi beat the heat, the inhuman humidity, and an old friend, Tommy Jacobs.

Winning the Open requires restraint of personality, suppression of emotion, and heaps of valor and maturity. When Venturi won, he had to overcome pain, dehydration, and daily temperatures hotter than Pensacola pavement in July. "I still believe winning the Open was a miracle," he says. "I was dead broke at the time. I'd sold everything I owned to remain on the Tour."

Venturi regularly stares at his replica of the trophy, a monument to his fortitude, a reminder of his glorious past. In 1956, he almost won the Masters as an amateur; then after qualifying for the professional tour in 1957, he won ten tournaments in four seasons.

Until injuries began ambushing him in the early 1960s, Venturi was one of the best professional golfers on Earth, nearly eye-to-eye with Palmer, Player, Casper, and Nicklaus. Golf supposedly bruises nothing except the ego, but years of belting balls toward holes in the ground, wrenching jolts to the body, can weaken the back, the fragile fulcrum of the game.

In 1961 Venturi hurt his back badly while bending down to retrieve his ball from the cup at a pro-am tournament in Palm Springs, California. In 1962 he hurt his wrists in an automobile accident. Golfers rely on their wrists more than the advice of their caddies; sturdy wrists are the rocket boosters of golf, the sources of power that induce shots to take off, to soar.

Men with wounds or doubts about their game usually bypass the Open, but Venturi had been playing well beforehand, so he came to Congressional Country Club enthusiastically. The field spent three days competing in smothering,

hot-house conditions. Venturi led Jacobs through fifty-two holes, but by then he was golfing with an empty canteen of sorts. The heat had wrung him dry and although he shot 66 in the third round, Venturi lost his lead with bogeys at the seventeenth and eighteenth holes. He stood at 208, two shots behind Jacobs.

The round had been a test of the golfers' stamina and the effectiveness of their deodorants. Venturi had barely enough reserve energy to totter to the locker room, his recovery room. He revived himself there with cups of tea and several salt tablets.

Venturi began the championship round unspectacularly with five pars and one bogey, but Jacobs and he were leading the tournament together because Jacobs had lost two shots at the second hole and another at the fourth. When he went out in 35 Venturi sure did look like an unlikely champion. His

lead on Jacobs had grown to two shots, yet skeptics were wondering whether Venturi had the physical and psychological strength to pass the finish line standing up.

The thermostat continually rose on the course…reaching 95, 97, 100 degrees Farenheit. Venturi, golfing on fumes, somehow found fuel in an empty tank. When pars were as meaningful as birdies, he made three in succession at the tenth, eleventh, and twelfth holes, the first from fifteen feet. At the thirteenth hole he put four shots between Jacobs and himself with a birdie from twenty feet.

When Venturi, who was trudging around the course like a thirsty tourist hopelessly lost in the Sahara, finally sank his par putt from ten feet at the eighteenth hole, he dropped his putter, grinned disbelievingly, raised his weary arms, and jubilantly declared: "My God, I've won the Open."

He went directly to the scorers' tent but did not sign his scorecard immediately. Perhaps he thought he was hallucinating, or maybe he thought his score was a mirage. "I remember staring and staring at the card," he says. "I couldn't remember one shot I'd hit. I was scared to death to sign the card, scared to death of being disqualified. Signing an incorrect scorecard was the only way I could lose the Open."

He says a voice from beyond (well, a voice from behind, anyway) told him to scribble his signature on the card. "One of the USGA officials, Joe Dey, who'd been looking over one of my shoulders, said, 'Sign the card, Ken. It's correct.'"

Venturi shot 70 in the fourth round, 278 overall, and wound up four strokes ahead of Jacobs. More than the title, however, Venturi cherishes Jacobs' reaction afterward. "I remember sitting on a bench talking about the finish of the tournament with [sportscaster] Bud Palmer. Tommy walks by and I tell him: 'Friend, if it couldn't be me I wish it were you.' He says: 'No, it should've been you.' That's the classiest remark I've ever heard."

He won five more tournaments in four years—the last at Harding Park in San Francisco, California, his practice tee years before—but retired to the television booth in 1968 because of the wrist injuries.

Although his Open victory is nearly thirty years old, Venturi still carries the memory of it with him as though it were an essential accessory, like his wallet.

AP/Wide World Photos

1 9 6 5

BELLERIVE COUNTRY CLUB
ST. LOUIS · MISSOURI

As the U.S. Open evolved, the USGA stuck to its notion that endurance was an important quality in a champion. The closing thirty-six holes that were played on Saturday often made for terrific theater; Ben Hogan's struggle to finish in 1950 wouldn't have been as dramatic if he had played only half as many holes. Just the year before, at Congressional Country Club, Ken Venturi had fought exhaustion to win in memorable fashion.

Despite these epic finishes, the USGA was forced to confront financial reality in 1965. The USGA turned to television. In today's athletic arena, television routinely dictates when and where games will be played, but until the mid-1960s, television was subservient to the events it covered. Then the amount of money involved increased considerably. The television people asked to spread the four rounds over four days, thereby filling another day with coverage and, consequently, selling more advertising time. Sensing greater rights fees, the USGA capitulated. In truth, the thirty-six-hole Saturday was a logistical nightmare. Any kind of weather interruption on Friday posed enormous problems on an already crowded Saturday.

The Bellerive Country Club course, exceedingly young by Open standards, featured large, easy-to-reach greens and therefore placed a premium on putting. One of the best golfers with the blade was Gary Player, a South African who was just approaching his prime at the age of twenty-nine. Player was relatively small, at five feet seven inches and 155 pounds, but he had won the British Open six years earlier and seemed at his best in championship events.

Player shot a 70 in the opening round, then matched it in the second. He maintained his lead in the third round with a 71. Player's nerves didn't show until he reached the sixteenth hole during Sunday's round. His double-bogey there, combined with Kel Nagle's birdie a hole ahead, left the two golfers tied at 282 after four rounds. Player went out quickly in the playoff, opening up a five-stroke lead on the front nine. Nagle's drives were often wild and he was no match for the steady, intense Player. Player won the playoff 71 to 74. He was the first non-American golfer to win the championship since Ted Ray of Britain in 1920.

Player's purse that year was $25,000, a far cry from the $150 Horace Rawlins collected for winning the Open at Newport seventy years earlier. Player, never a conformist on any level, gave away all of his prize money. The USGA was happy to accept $20,000 to continue its work in the area of junior golf. An additional $5,000 was awarded to cancer research.

In a career that spanned the world, this was Player's only U.S. Open title. He would win the Masters and the British Open three times each, and the PGA Championship twice. To this day, Player is the only foreign golfer to win the four major titles. The other three to achieve that feat are Gene Sarazen, Ben Hogan, and Jack Nicklaus.

OPPOSITE PAGE: *Gary Player dances a jig after an important putt.* ABOVE: *Kel Nagle* (LEFT) *and Gary Player clasp hands after tying at 282 in the fourth round of the 1965 Open.*

1 9 6 6

OLYMPIC CLUB
SAN FRANCISCO · CALIFORNIA

By now, Arnold Palmer's brilliant career had crested. The early 1960s had been his, and his alone. In 1960, with eight tournament victories, he led all golfers. In 1961 he and Doug Sanders each led with five wins. In 1962 and 1963, Palmer was all alone with seven titles. Palmer won six of his eight major titles in that span of four years, including the 1960 U.S. Open, when he came from seven strokes back. The last major title had been the 1964 Masters, and with the emergence of Jack Nicklaus and Billy Casper, Palmer and his fans wondered if he would ever elevate his game to that level again.

Palmer was thirty-six years old when the world's best professional golfers gathered at Olympic Club in 1966. He was the sentimental choice of many, but Nicklaus and Casper were the real favorites. Between the years of 1964 and 1968, either Nicklaus or Casper led all money winners and won the most tournaments each season. Palmer, ever the aggressor, didn't fare well on Olympic's testing front nine. At the first round's

AP/Wide World Photos

midpoint, his score was a dismal 38. Palmer rallied, though, and finished with a 71, four strokes off the pace.

Momentum is a phenomenon usually noted in games like football or soccer, but it might be a more important factor in golf. After all, a golfer is an individual; his play is often a product of his confidence level. Palmer began to feel the old magic at Olympic late in his first round. He dismantled the course the second day with a searing 66. His putting ability, which had eroded in recent years, prevented him from tying Rives McBee's record-matching 64. Palmer blew two putts that were shorter than five feet on the last two holes. As it was, he was tied for the lead at 137 with Casper. The two classic golfers were paired together for round three.

Palmer won the first head-to-head battle, shooting a 70, while Casper seemed sluggish on his way to a 73. As the two low golfers, Palmer and Casper played together again in the fourth round. It was all over, or so it seemed, after nine holes. Palmer, charging at every opportunity, fired a sensational 32 on the front nine. Casper, who tooled around in a modest 36, trailed by a hopeless seven strokes. Nicklaus was nine shots back and Palmer was all by himself.

In truth, he was not alone. For Palmer was an ardent student of the game's history and he knew he was traveling toward uncharted waters. Back in 1948, Ben Hogan had riddled the Riviera Country Club in Los Angeles, winning the U.S. Open with a record score of 276. As he moved to the tenth tee, Palmer did the arithmetic: he needed a 36 over the final nine holes, a pedestrian one over par, to finish with a new championship record of 275.

Casper, unaware of Palmer's lofty goal, figured it was over. He had been playing well since a Chicago doctor discovered he was allergic to a number of common foods. Casper's bulging waistline was now under control, and his swing was sweeter than ever. Casper, a week shy of his thirty-fifth birthday, didn't want to embarrass himself. He vowed silently to play consistent golf over the final nine, painfully aware that he was seven strokes behind with nine holes to play.

OPPOSITE PAGE: *Billy Casper's amazing come-from-behind victory over Arnold Palmer in 1966 had its rough spots; this one was at the seventh hole of round three.*

Casper's par on the tenth hole was routine enough. No one really thought much of it, even in light of Palmer's uncharacteristic bogey, because the lead was still six shots. Both men parred the eleventh hole, then Casper birdied the twelfth. Then again, so did Palmer, whose 1966 U.S. Open was beginning to take on a Hoganesque tinge. It was now a six-shot lead with six holes to play. Confidently firing at the flag on the par-three thirteenth, Palmer missed the green entirely and was reduced to taking a bogey. Casper, meanwhile, plodded on with a par. Five shots, five holes.

After both men parred the fourteenth, Palmer was blinded again by history. Knowing he needed to play the last four holes in even par to beat Hogan's record and aware that the hardest holes were yet to come, Palmer decided to go for birdie on the fifteenth hole. His iron shot found the sand, though, and he recorded his second bogey in three holes. Casper, sensing for the first time that he had a chance, rolled in his birdie putt. Three shots, three holes.

By now Palmer knew that beating Hogan would be difficult. The way Casper was putting, even winning the U.S. Open might not be easy. Palmer immediately backed himself against the wall when his tee shot on the majestic par-five sixteenth hole hooked sharply into the considerable rough. Palmer's aggressiveness rarely betrayed him, but now he elected to recover with a stiff three-iron. His second shot found the rough on the other side of the fairway. Palmer grimaced and chipped back onto the fairway. His blast to the green fell short, right into a sand trap. Palmer, calling on all his skills, managed to get home in two more shots. Still, it was a six and Casper, his putter searing hot, had slyly scored birdie. Astonishingly, Palmer's seemingly insurmountable seven-shot lead was down to a single stroke.

By now, Casper's surge to the top seemed inevitable. On the seventeenth, he caught Palmer, or rather, Palmer fell back even with Casper. Once again, Palmer's tee shot hooked into the rough guarding the left side of the narrow fairway and his recovery dribbled into the right rough. He actually had an opportunity to make par, but his ten-foot putt just slid past the cup. Casper made a routine par and with one hole to go the 1966 U.S. Open was even; Casper had come from seven strokes down in eight holes. When Palmer's first shot (he had switched to a safer iron off the tee) hooked for the third consecutive time, it looked like Casper's championship. But then a curious thing happened. Palmer, who had seen his game vanish completely, summoned one last, great shot. Tearing through the thick grass, he muscled a marvelous wedge shot that soared all the way to the back of the green. Palmer rolled his thirty-foot putt over the treacherously fast green some six feet past the hole. Putting before Casper, Palmer willed the ball into the cup. Casper missed his long birdie putt and the two golfers were tied after seventy-two holes, at 278, two strokes off Hogan's eighteen-year-old record. Palmer's final round was an up-and-down 71, while Casper had responded to the pressure with a 32 over the final nine and a total of 68.

The eighteen-hole playoff the next day was more of the same: Palmer charged out to a two-stroke lead over the front nine and then watched as slowly, inexorably, his hard-earned margin melted away. The score was even after the eleventh hole, when Casper's putter scored again; he birdied while Palmer bogeyed. The par-three thirteenth hole was the tournament in microcosm. Palmer struggled for a routine par, and Casper coaxed a fifty-foot putt into the hole for a birdie and his first lead. When it was over, Casper, 69, had throttled Palmer, 73. The secret to Casper's success? On ninety testing holes, he didn't have to three-putt even once.

Palmer still had the stuff to win on the professional tour. Between 1966 and 1973, he would win seventeen more tournaments, running his total up to sixty, fourth on the all-time list behind Sam Snead, Jack Nicklaus, and Ben Hogan. None of those victories, however, would be majors.

1 9 6 7

BALTUSROL GOLF CLUB
SPRINGFIELD · NEW JERSEY

By 1967, Jack Nicklaus was at the peak of his powers. Since turning professional in 1962, he had placed among the tour's four top money winners in each of six years, a streak that would carry him through an additional eleven years. From the beginning, Nicklaus had made it clear that winning major tournaments was his primary objective. He has been more than a

little successful. The reason? Attitude. "Believe it or not," he says today, "the majors are the easiest tournaments of the year to win. I figure if I hang in there, just stay around the top, people are going to fall back because they can't handle the pressure."

The Golden Bear could handle the pressure. He had won the U.S. Amateur in 1959 and 1961 and then christened his rookie season with a victory in the 1962 U.S. Open. When Nicklaus was preparing for Baltusrol's Lower Course in 1967, he had already added three Masters titles, a British Open victory, and a PGA championship to the list.

Despite a horrific (for him, anyway) string of performances earlier in the spring, Nicklaus was the odds-on favorite in the rolling hills of New Jersey. Arnold Palmer, of course, was again the people's choice. His lone Open win had come seven years earlier at Cherry Hills, but he was usually near the top of the leaderboard in the nation's championship. His disastrous loss at Olympic left him hungry to prove himself again. Baltusrol, though, had developed a reputation for producing less-than-predictable champions. After the immortal Willie Anderson won there in 1903, the U.S. Open winners at Baltusrol were golfers named Jerome Travers, Tony Manero, and Ed Furgol.

Sure enough, the leader after the first day was a twenty-three-year-old amateur named Marty Fleckman. He blistered Baltusrol with a 67; there had been three weeks without rain before the tournament, and the rough was not up to the USGA's exacting standards. Palmer and Deane Beman, the longtime amateur who had finally turned professional earlier that year, were in a group of six golfers two strokes back.

Despite a first-round 71, Nicklaus remained convinced that the tournament winner had a chance to beat Ben Hogan's record of 276, set in 1948 at Riviera. The course was playing reasonably long at 7,015 yards, but the greens and fairways were in exceptional condition. With the thinner-than-usual rough, the warm temperatures, and the lack of any significant wind, the course seemed ready to yield low scores. Palmer came back with a 68 the second day for a total of 137, good enough to lead at the midpoint. Nicklaus, who started his second round at about the time Palmer finished, began badly by taking a bogey on the first hole. Then, he left himself an eleven-foot putt for par on the picturesque fourth hole. Nicklaus, using a Bull's Eye putter loaned to him by Fred

Mueller, sank the challenging putt and turned his round around in the process. Nicklaus birdied the fifth and eighth holes, then the twelfth, sixteenth, and eighteenth holes; this was good for a 67, one of the best rounds Nicklaus ever posted in U.S. Open competition. Thus, Nicklaus stood at 138, a stroke behind Palmer and one ahead of reigning champion Billy Casper. Fleckman, who had ballooned to a 73, was a stroke behind Casper.

All of this meant that Palmer, the legend, and Nicklaus, the heir to his throne, would be paired together on Saturday. The head-to-head matchup, however, did not produce the antici-pated results. Perhaps too conscious of each other, Nicklaus and Palmer struggled. Their drivers were unreliable and their putters cooled off. Nicklaus finished with a 72, while Palmer was a stroke back at 73. If they hadn't both birdied the final hole, it would have been worse. Meanwhile, the crafty Casper put together a string of birdies. With four holes left to play he had a four-stroke lead. Then Casper did the unthinkable: he bogeyed the fifteenth, sixteenth, and seventeenth holes. Now the leaderboard was a mess: Fleckman, who had rallied with a 69, led with a 209; Nicklaus, Palmer, and Casper, golf's ranking triumvirate, appropriately were in a three-way tie for second at 210; four more players, including Beman, were only two strokes off the pace.

Fleckman and Casper played in the final twosome, just behind Nicklaus and Palmer. Immediately, the pressure affected Fleckman's nerves. He bogeyed the first hole, then the second, the third, and the sixth. He toured the first nine holes in 38 and finished with an execrable 80. In the face of this, Casper was hardly inspired to play great golf. He never made a move. After the first nine holes, the two large galleries following the last two pairs merged as one. It had become clear that either Nicklaus or Palmer would win the U.S. Open, and the crowd's clear favorite was Palmer.

The turning point might have come as early as the second hole. Nicklaus dropped his second shot into the sand and blew a ten-foot putt for par. Palmer, on the other hand, was staring a twelve-foot birdie in the face. He missed, and a potential two-stroke lead was reduced to only one. Nicklaus, who had feared the worst, breathed a sigh of relief. He birdied the third hole with a crisp eight-iron to the green and a twelve-foot putt.

Nicklaus had the momentum now. His three-iron to the fourth green deposited the ball four feet from the cup. That birdie and Fleckman's errors gave Nicklaus the tournament lead. He pushed the margin to two strokes by birdying the fifth hole.

Nicklaus gave one back by bogeying the sixth hole, and Palmer seemed poised to move into a tie on the seventh. Palmer had drilled a one-iron to within twelve feet of the hole, while Nicklaus had been more cautious in his approach and now studied a twenty-two foot putt for birdie. He stroked it aggressively, and after a slight right-to-left break, it went in. The pro-Palmer crowd sighed. Palmer, perhaps unnerved, missed his putt by an inch. With eleven holes left, the U.S. Open was basi-cally over. Palmer took a five on the ninth hole and Nicklaus birdied to run his lead to four strokes. On the eighteenth hole, Nicklaus blistered a one-iron that just missed a bunker protect-ing the front of the green and stopped twenty-two feet from the hole.

"As I made the long walk up the hill, I knew I had that putt to beat Hogan's record," Nicklaus remembers. "I had the tour-nament won, that was the big thing, the only thing. I worked on the putt, of course, and I happened to make it. But records are just bonuses, the cherry on the sundae. The importance of my total was that it was the lowest in the 1967 United States Open."

Perhaps, but Nicklaus' birdie on the final hole gave him a remarkable round of 65 and a four-day aggregate of 275, one better than Hogan's nineteen-year-old record.

The luxurious grounds of Baltusrol Golf Club.

1 9 6 8

In retrospect, the final results at Baltusrol were instructive. Jack Nicklaus was first, followed in order by Arnold Palmer, Don January, and Billy Casper. In fifth place, on the strength of a closing round of 70, was Lee Buck Trevino, the grandson of a Mexican gravedigger. Only a week before, he had been employed as a professional at the Horizon Hills Country Club in El Paso, Texas. Trevino was twenty-seven, old for a newcomer, but he had qualified for the 1966 U.S. Open and placed a respectable fifty-fourth. His $6,000 winnings in the 1967 Open convinced him and backers in Texas that he might have a future in professional golf.

By 1968, Trevino was no longer an anonymous rookie. In fact, he had collected more than $50,000 in prize money by the time Oak Hill beckoned to him in mid-June. He was buoyed by the fact that his style of play, his oddly flat swing, and his low-trajectory shots were suited to the tight fairways and slick greens favored by the USGA.

"Nobody had ever seen a swing like mine," Trevino says today. "I could play the bump-and-run game that worked on those courses. I learned to play in Texas on greens where you couldn't stop the ball. You had to bounce it short of the green, then let it run. That style worked real well when the greens were wet. It's not a coincidence that most of my championships came on wet greens; I always did well in the mud. I could always stop a three- or four-iron on a wet green."

As it happened, rain had softened Oak Hill in 1968. Bert Yancey came out firing and produced rounds of 67 and 68 for a midpoint total of 135, equaling the tournament record. Trevino had kept pace by shooting 69 and 68. His third-round 69 brought him closer, because Yancey eased up with a 70. The standings after three rounds were Yancey at 205, Trevino at 206, and Nicklaus and Charles Coody at 212.

Compared to the other leaders, Trevino was almost an afterthought. "No one knew who I was," Trevino says. "I remember finishing my rounds and sitting in a cart outside the pro shop, near the putting green. I was drinking a few beers,

looking for someone to talk to. No one asked for an autograph, no one stopped to talk. They thought I was the cart man."

The pressure of the U.S. Open, particularly if you are in contention in the final round, is intense. How many marginal golfers have found themselves close to the lead late in the proceedings, only to self-destruct? Earlier that season, Trevino had faded badly under pressure in the Masters and the Houston Open. People wondered when he would begin to crack. In truth, Trevino was exceptionally nervous. He just didn't show it.

"I was talking, joking, having a good time," Trevino says. "But inside I'm grinding, I'm grinding, really nervous. It's like walking in the cemetery and whistling. When I was six or seven I'd go with my grandfather to the graveyard. He watered it at night. It was pitch black and you could hear your footsteps against the tombstones. I learned not to be afraid at an early age.

"The advantage I had over guys like Nicklaus and Yancey was that I had nothing to lose. Hell, I wasn't even supposed to be there. They had everything to lose. The press asked me after the third round if I thought I could win. I said, 'Sure, I've got a better shot than them.' But they already had their headlines written."

Trevino started badly, sculling his shot off the first tee, then backed up his words. He passed Yancey on the ninth hole, then buried him on the eleventh and twelfth holes. Trevino, never one to linger over a putt, showed no sign of nerves. He walked up to a thirty-foot putt on eleven and drilled it into the cup. "No one expects to make a thirty-foot putt," Trevino says, "but you have to give it a chance. That putt was hit pretty hard. I was a little lucky. It probably would have gone four or five feet past the hole. Then I would have had one of those little downhill sliders and who knows what would have happened."

On the twelfth, Trevino knocked in a slightly uphill putt of twenty-two feet. By now, Yancey was five strokes back. Only a charging Nicklaus, who shot a closing 67, made it moderately interesting. Trevino needed to birdie the final hole to break Nicklaus' U.S. Open record of 275, but he hooked his drive into the left rough and scrambled for par and a share of the mark. Trevino's last round in the crucible of the Open was an impressive 69, making him the first golfer to shoot all four rounds under par and all four rounds in the 60s.

All week long at Oak Hill, Lee Trevino seemed to walk on air. With four dazzling rounds in the 60s, Trevino held off Jack Nicklaus and Bert Yancey to win his first U.S. Open in 1968.

Orville Moody finally wrapped up the 1969 Open at Champions with a consistent 72 in the final round. Moody was an Army sergeant who was artful off the tee, but frighteningly inconsistent around the greens.

AP/Wide World Photos

1 9 6 9

Over the years the U.S. Open has produced some unlikely champions. Sam Parks, who stunned the Oakmont field in 1935, is arguably the biggest surprise in nearly a century of national championships. Orville Moody is a close second.

Moody was thirty-five years old when he qualified for the U.S. Open at Champions. He had never won a tournament on the professional tour, mostly because he hadn't spent any significant time on the tour. For fourteen years, Moody toiled in the U.S. Army. The Oklahoman rose to the rank of sergeant and headed maintenance and supervision of all Army golf courses. His game was not exactly balanced: Moody was a marvelous striker of the ball, but when he reached the green his putting almost always betrayed him.

Moody began modestly enough, shooting a 71 in the first round. That placed him five strokes behind torrid Bob Murphy and four in back of Miller Barber. It was Barber who led the steamy tournament after three rounds with a total of 206, three strokes better than Moody, who had found an equilibrium and followed his 71 with rounds of 70 and 68. Barber blew up early in the fourth round, throwing away four strokes over the first six holes. Moody, steady as ever, shot a 35 over the front nine to take a one-stroke lead. Slowly, strangely, the familiar names fell from grace. Arnold Palmer, Al Geiberger, Deane Beman, and Bob Rosburg all backed up, and there was Moody walking up the eighteenth fairway needing only a par to win his first tournament. His gentle eight-iron left him a fifteen-foot putt for birdie and though he missed it, Moody easily rolled in a short putt for a 281 total and the championship.

It was the only title Moody would ever win. Over his curious career, Moody won $389,915 on the tour, but at the age of fifty he found a new life on the PGA Seniors Tour. Through 1991, Moody had won nine senior events and amassed more than $2 million in winnings.

Orville Moody blasts out of the twelfth-hole rough at Champions Golf Club during the 1969 Open.

1 9 7 0

HAZELTINE NATIONAL GOLF CLUB
CHASKA · MINNESOTA

England's Tony Jacklin had emerged as a championship golfer the season before, winning the 1969 British Open at the tender age of twenty-five. He immediately distinguished himself in the first round at Hazeltine the following year, shooting a 71. It was not, at first glance, a terribly impressive score, but it came with a perspective.

Hazeltine, a young course, was under seige even before the tournament began. The golfers viewed it as unfair, citing numerous blind shots. When the wind whipped up in time for the start, the course was close to unplayable. Playing in winds that approached forty miles an hour, Jacklin somehow found a way to master the course. His clever shots managed to stay on the greens and the result was six birdies. Jacklin was all alone with a three-stroke lead. Nearly half the field, including Jack Nicklaus, scored an 80 or higher; it was the Golden Bear's worst Open score to date.

The second round was more conventional. Jacklin's 70 gave him a 141 total, two strokes ahead of Dave Hill, who shot a second-day 69. It was the blunt-talking Hill who blistered the course after his round, saying, "Plow it up and start over. They ruined a good farm when they built this course."

That was as aggressive as Hill got the rest of the way. He was fined by the USGA for his candor. Jacklin's 70 gave him a four-stroke lead heading into the final round. To be sure, Jacklin tightened up down the stretch. He bogeyed the seventh and eighth holes. There might have been a third consecutive bogey, but for an incredible stroke of luck. Jacklin's twenty-five-foot bid for a birdie was hit far too boldly and seemed destined to run well past the cup, but it crashed into the back of the hole, bounced well over it, and dropped back in. It was a two-shot bounce, and Jacklin never faltered thereafter. He finished with his third 70 in a row and posted a total of 281. Hill was seven strokes behind in second, one of the widest margins in the tournament's history. Jacklin's sense of timing was precise; exactly fifty years before, fellow Englishman Ted Ray had won the U.S. Open, the last time the English received that distinction.

Bob Thomas Sports Photography

Bob Thomas Sports Photography

OPPOSITE PAGE: *Tony Jacklin won the 1970 Open at Hazeltine National Golf Club, marking the first English victory in fifty years.* LEFT: *Showing a deft touch with his putter, Tony Jacklin took a four-stroke lead into the final round at Hazeltine and escaped with a 70 on the final day. He finished with a 281 total and his only Open triumph on this side of the Atlantic.*

1 9 7 1

While Trevino had been something of a surprise winner at the 1968 U.S. Open, he didn't sneak up on anyone at Merion three years later. By now Trevino, along with Jack Nicklaus and Billy Casper, was one of the world's most distinguished golfers. He had won six tournaments since Oak Hill and been the professional tour's most efficient golfer in 1970, winning the Vardon Trophy for best strokes-per-round average. Like history's finest golfers, Trevino was at his best when it mattered most. Although Nicklaus was the golfer to beat at Merion, that wasn't how Trevino saw it. "If anything I was overconfident," Trevino says. "I was making a lot of money, almost too easily. I was drinking too much, keeping late hours. I didn't stay in the kind of shape that I should have. The best thing that happened to my career was getting hit by lightning in 1975."

That would be four years later, but there was plenty of thunder in the course at Merion, one of the toughest in memory. It was a par-seventy course that played only 6,544 yards, but seemed a lot longer. Trevino was among those who considered Merion the toughest layout they had ever seen. Unlike Hazeltine, the maligned course from the year before, Merion was discussed in reverent tones. Breaking par over four rounds would be exceptionally difficult.

Someone named Labron Harris opened with a 67, however, leaving people to question Merion's reputation. Nicklaus, true to form, was only two strokes back with a 69. Trevino shot a modest 70. Both men shot 72s the next day to fall further off the 138 pace set by Jim Colbert and Bob Erikson. The third round belonged to amateur Jim Simons, who performed surgery on Merion's testing course and shot a remarkable seven-birdie 65, for a fifty-four-hole total of 207. Simons did this in plain view of Trevino, who as his playing partner shot a relatively plain 69. Nicklaus' 68 left him two strokes back, two ahead of Trevino.

On Sunday, Simons was paired with Nicklaus, the other heavy hitter. Predictably, the twenty-one-year-old wilted under pressure. He took a 38 on the front nine and matched it on the back side for a 76. Both Trevino and Nicklaus almost let the tournament slip away on the few final elegant holes. Trevino's putter was just good enough, though, and he shot a 69 to finish the four rounds at 280. On the last hole, Nicklaus had a fifteen-foot putt for a birdie and his third U.S. Open victory. He pondered the shot, then sent a firm putt toward the hole. It slid past the right side and Nicklaus finished with a 72, a score that tied Trevino and forced an eighteen-hole playoff the next day.

Trevino always seemed to master the par-threes in championship settings. His philosophy was quite simple. "Don't take any bogeys on the par-threes, try to birdie the par-fives, and the par-fours will take care of themselves," Trevino says. "Good drives are important. You have to be on the green to have a chance. It's like dogs chasing cars and pros putting for cars— eventually, they're going to die.

"You have to think positive on those putts, it's the key. Two things can happen when you putt: it can go in or stay out. That's it. Too many of these guys look like there's a double-barrel shotgun at their heads when they face these little four- and five-footers. Nothing bad like that is going to happen. A miss is just a miss."

Trevino, whose glib manner masked the approach of a scientist, was a little tight as the two giants teed off. Trevino hit one bad shot in the entire round with Nicklaus, an ill-aimed nine-iron that found sand on the first hole. He bogeyed, giving Nicklaus a short-lived lead. Trevino settled down and it was Nicklaus who struck a pair of unartful shots. He needed two shots to escape a bunker on the second hole and took a bogey, then lost two more strokes to par on the third. Trevino had played those two holes in even par, making a one-stroke deficit turn into a two-stroke lead. Nicklaus rallied, but Trevino's guile on the green won the match-play playoff after the turn for home.

Trevino coaxed home a difficult twenty-five-foot birdie putt on the twelfth hole, then saved his par on the fourteenth with a ten-footer. He made another twenty-five-foot birdie putt on the fifteenth hole, and it was over. Trevino won with a 68, com-

OPPOSITE PAGE: *Lee Trevino didn't appear to have the patience for championship golf. He seemed to address the ball as he approached it, and before one could blink an eye, it was gone. Here, on his way to a second U.S. Open victory, he cranks up at Merion in 1971.*

Bob Thomas Sports Photography

pared to Nicklaus' 71. It was Trevino's second U.S Open title in four years, and his remarkable championship form held for most of the summer. In a span of twenty-three days, he also won the Canadian Open and the British Open, the latter at Royal Birkdale.

"It's funny," Trevino says. "I can remember everything about those championships. Everything. Shots you hit, people you were with. I can't always tell you what year it was, but I remember everything else. It's hard to believe it was more than twenty years ago.

"Yes, I'm proud of my two U.S. Opens. A lot of great golfers never won one, like Sam Snead. I was lucky, but I worked hard, too. Championships like that, you just take them when they come."

AP/Wide World Photos

PEBBLE BEACH GOLF LINKS
PEBBLE BEACH · CALIFORNIA

Jack Nicklaus took the playoff defeat at Merion quite hard. He was in position to win the 1971 British Open as well, but Trevino had beaten him there, too. The 1972 season was Nicklaus' eleventh as a professional and he already had amassed twelve major titles, but the near-misses left him frustrated. Pebble Beach was a venue Nicklaus enjoyed; he had won a pair of Bing Crosby tournaments there, as well as his 1961 U.S. Amateur title.

Nicklaus wasn't shy in the first round. He came out firing and finished with a 71 over the seaside course. Unfortunately, there were five other golfers tied with him for the lead, an Open record. The scary thing was that Nicklaus' putter had betrayed him again and again. He missed five reasonable putts, all of them potential par-breakers. The second round wasn't any better. Nicklaus shot a 73 and there on the leaderboard were six men tied for the midpoint lead with an aggregate total of 144. Arnold Palmer, who had opened with a 77, shot a 68 and crept to within one shot of the lead. Clearly, though, Pebble Beach was winning the battle.

It was more of the same in the third round. Nicklaus shot a 72, giving him an even-par 216 through fifty-four holes. Trevino, who was still suffering the aftereffects of a bout with pneumonia, rallied with four birdies on the back nine and trailed Nicklaus by a stroke. Palmer, Kermit Zarley, and Bruce Crampton were two shots off the lead. Nicklaus and Trevino were paired together for the final round for the second consecutive year, but they didn't produce a classic duel. Trevino just wasn't up to it.

Pebble Beach is not exactly the place to stray from the straight and narrow, but Jack Nicklaus (LEFT) salvaged this errant shot on the first hole, ultimately winning his third U.S. Open. There was a time on the back nine of the final round that Arnold Palmer seemed to have the Open at Pebble Beach (OPPOSITE PAGE) in hand, but by the time the golfers reached the gorgeous eighteenth hole of the course, Jack Nicklaus had wrapped the tournament up.

The second hole underlined the gap between the two golfers that day. Nicklaus scored a birdie and Trevino bogeyed. He trailed by three shots. Though Nicklaus got careless, he managed to complete the first nine holes in even par, good enough for a four-stroke lead over Trevino, Palmer, and Crampton. Just when it looked like Nicklaus would coast in, he sent his wind-blown drive on the tenth hole sailing over the adjacent cliff and down onto the beach. The result was a double-bogey; his lead was halved. It was down to a scant stroke when Nicklaus and Palmer simultaneously eyed eight-foot putts that would determine the championship. Palmer, playing two holes ahead of Nicklaus, was looking at a birdie on the fourteenth. Nicklaus, who had lost a stroke in the rough behind the twelfth green, needed his putt for bogey. With the right combination, Palmer, at age forty-two, would be leading the tournament by one shot. But Nicklaus, ten years younger, had the nerve to make that delicate putt when Palmer did not. Thus, Palmer trailed by a stroke and fell apart down the stretch. Nicklaus, playing cautiously with a big lead, finished with a 74 and an aggregate of 290, two strokes over par and three ahead of second-place finisher Bruce Crampton.

Nicklaus now had three U.S. Opens to his credit and thirteen major tournament wins, almost tying him with the great Bobby Jones.

OAKMONT COUNTRY CLUB
OAKMONT · PENNSYLVANIA

As the decades passed, Oakmont became a U.S. Open fixture. It was perhaps the most difficult venue golfers faced and, at the same time, was consistently the best-prepared. H. C. Fownes, an amateur golfer of some distinction, had begun carving out the course in a Pittsburgh suburb seventy years earlier. It was long and it boasted the slickest greens in the nation. So dastardly was the course that in 1973 the USGA actually widened two of the narrow fairways. This U.S. Open would be the fifth championship tournament for Oakmont, tying it with Baltusrol for the record.

Nicklaus, quite naturally, was the favorite. He had, after all, won the previous year at Pebble Beach and was at the peak of his career. The press didn't dwell on the presence of Johnny Miller, a blond Californian, who had won two tournaments in five years on the professional tour. Not that Miller didn't have a track record of note in the Open. In 1966, at the age of nineteen, Miller qualified for the U.S. Open at Olympic and finished in a tie for eighth. He had placed seventh at Merion two years before. Miller had a sweet swing and his irons, when his game was on, were lethal. His putter, too, could carry him. The problem with Miller was his emotions. Sometimes, the pressure was too much for him to handle.

Still, Miller's game was perfectly suited to Oakmont. His practice rounds buoyed his spirit, and two days before the first round a psychic told him he would win. Why not, he thought to himself? When Miller learned that he would be paired with Arnold Palmer he was both excited and apprehensive. He relished the head-to-head challenge, but he had seen how badly Arnie's Army had treated Nicklaus at Baltusrol in 1967.

The only golfer to master the course in the opening round was the meticulous Gary Player. The South African shot a 67, three strokes better than the trio of Lee Trevino, Ray Floyd, and Jim Colbert. They were the only ones under par, as Oakmont rose to the occasion. Miller and Palmer each shot a modest 71. Then something peculiar happened. Oakmont found itself laid bare. It had been a rainy spring and the course was holding

water. Officials, pleased with the quickness of the greens in the first round, advised course employees to water the greens for five minutes between rounds. Later, golfers wondered if the sprinklers had inadvertently been left on for too long.

It didn't take the golfers long to realize that they wouldn't be penalized for aiming their irons directly at the flag stick. The greens were invitingly soft and Friday's round was merely target golf. Gene Borek, a club professional from Long Island, fired a startling round of 65. In all, twenty-seven golfers broke par. Player's 70 gave him a 137 and a one-stroke lead over Colbert. Miller, who fashioned a second-round 69, was tied with Nicklaus for a third at 140. Palmer's second 71 gave him a 142.

It rained early Saturday morning, ending any chance for the greens to dry and quicken. Player opened the tournament to a dozen competitors by shooting a 77 in the third round. Now there were four golfers tied for the lead going into the final eighteen holes: Palmer, Julius Boros, John Schlee, and Jerry Heard. There were four more men within two strokes. Miller was not one of them. He had forgotten his yardage card and was five over after seven holes. His wife drove back to the hotel to retrieve the card and Miller played the rest of the round even. Nonetheless, the damage had been done; Miller's score of 76 put him six strokes back, and, he thought, out of the tournament.

Miller took out his frustration on the practice tee. It didn't go well. He had five balls left when a voice, a voice of authority, stopped him in mid-swing. "This is weird, I know," Miller remembers, "but this voice says to me, 'Open your stance way up.' I looked around really quick and said, 'Who said that?' I guess it was just a strong statement from somewhere in my brain, but I tried it. At that point I'd have tried anything."

Miller opened his stance, which cut down his considerable backswing slightly and allowed him to play more of a fade. The last five swings felt terrific, and Miller wondered as he walked to the putting green if he should stay with the radical change. When he awoke the next morning, he decided to try the open stance. He was partnered with Miller Barber in the final round and teed off in the eighth-to-last pair six shots behind the leader and three over par. What happened next approached the fantastic.

On the first hole, Miller rifled his drive down the middle and his five-iron deposited the ball five feet from the hole. Birdie.

Johnny Miller, seen here at the
1971 Masters in Augusta, Georgia,
was one of the most promising
young golfers of his day.

Photofest

Miller's nine-iron at the second hole almost flew in the hole, but stopped six inches away. Birdie. On the third hole, it was a drive and a muscular five-iron to within twenty-five feet of the hole. Birdie. On the fourth hole, a long par-five, Miller hit two big drives, blasted out of the sand, and set up another short putt. Birdie. In four holes Miller had picked up four strokes. He was two strokes behind the leaders and one under par for the tournament. Miller fully understood that the stakes had suddenly changed. "Geez, I'm in the hunt," Miller mused as he walked to the fifth tee. "I could win this thing. Those leaders, they're going to start choking their guts out."

Of course, it was Miller who began to choke. He parred the fifth, sixth, and seventh holes, then three-putted on the eighth green for a bogey. "I went from being nervous to being semi-mad," Miller says. "That kind of got me focused again."

Miller put together two good shots, a drive and a two-iron, on the par-five ninth and got down in a two-putt from forty feet. Birdie. Through nine holes, Miller had scored a 32, but the leaders weren't backing up. The gallery around Miller and Barber began to swell as news of Miller's round circulated. After a routine par on the tenth hole, Miller fell into another unconscious groove. He birdied the eleventh with a fourteen-foot

putt, birdied the twelfth with a fifteen-foot putt, then birdied the thirteenth with a laser of a four-iron and a five-foot putt. That gave Miller a round of seven under, four under overall, and vaulted him into a tie for the lead with Palmer. Miller just missed a twelve-foot putt on the fourteenth for another birdie, but came right back to beat one of the world's toughest holes. The par-four, 453-yard fifteenth demanded near perfection and that is what Miller offered. A drive and a sizzling four-iron gave him a ten-foot birdie putt. It dropped. Now Miller was eight under par and a stroke ahead of Palmer.

This was news to Palmer, who felt he was in control of the tournament, even at the age of forty-three. Schlee, Boros, and Tom Weiskopf were all a stroke behind him. Who else could be in it? Palmer pitched to within four feet of the eleventh hole and a true putt would push him to five under. Palmer missed, then cursed when he saw Miller's name on the leaderboard. He was behind when he had thought he was ahead. Palmer promptly bogeyed the next three holes and fell out of contention.

Miller, meanwhile, parred the last three holes to finish the back nine in 31 strokes, giving him an unheard of 63, the lowest round ever shot in a U.S. Open. Frighteningly enough, it could have been a 61. Miller's putt for birdie on seventeen had lipped out, and his bid at eighteen was too strong and bounced out of the cup. Miller had hit every green, all but one fairway, and averaged nine feet for each of his staggering nine birdies. He was confident his 279 would hold up, and it did. Schlee's fifty-foot chip from the rough swung wide, and Weiskopf couldn't eagle the final hole, leaving Miller as the champion.

For the next two years, Miller was the world's best golfer. He led the tour in earnings in 1974. His eight tournament victories that season were the most since Palmer's 1960 season. Miller would win the 1976 British Open for his second major, and when his career was over he had won twenty-three titles. It was his final eighteen holes at Oakmont, however, that made golf history. Was it the finest round ever played under pressure? Palmer's 65 had brought him from seven strokes back in the 1960 Open at Cherry Hills. Ben Hogan won at Oakland Hills in 1951 with a stirring 67. Historians downplay Miller's round, pointing to the course's vulnerable greens.

Miller shrugs. "Well, it was a little soft," he says. "But it was still Oakmont."

OPPOSITE PAGE: *Oakmont Country Club is one of the most frequently used courses in Open history.* ABOVE: *Johnny Miller sinks his par-four putt on the eighteenth and final hole at Oakmont to record his masterful 63. His total of 279 held up as the best aggregate of the 1973 U.S. Open.*

Hale Irwin (ABOVE) *looked suitably impressed when he held the U.S. Open Trophy aloft in 1974. He won at Winged Foot, despite a score of seven shots over par. The 1975 Open was a close contest, but Lou Graham* (OPPOSITE PAGE) *eventually landed the much-coveted prize.*

1 9 7 4

WINGED FOOT GOLF CLUB
MAMARONECK · NEW YORK

The USGA had been more than a little humbled by Johnny Miller's final round at Oakmont the year before. Shooting a 63 on a testing U.S. Open course just wasn't permitted. Winged Foot, therefore, was the perfect comeback for the USGA. George Fazio had added a little length to the par-four holes on the classic course. It was long, it was tight, the greens were like glass. Winged Foot was nearly unplayable compared to the lush, sprawling courses the professionals were accustomed to.

The course demanded accuracy off the tee and a deft touch with the long irons to the green. Putting was also a critical part of the equation. The first round was an unmitigated disaster as far as the golfers were concerned. Miller, for instance, shot an unflattering 76. Gary Player, usually a factor in major tournaments, managed to fashion a 70 for the first-round lead. He slipped to a 73 in the second round and into a tie for the lead, at 143, with Arnold Palmer, Ray Floyd, and Hale Irwin. Irwin was the group's curiosity. He had won two tournaments in six years on the tour, the Heritage Classic both times, had played football for the University of Colorado, and had won the National Collegiate Athletic Association (NCAA) golf title in 1967. Irwin was not a charismatic player; he wore glasses and hit straight off the tee. Long irons and staying out of trouble were his specialties.

Tom Watson crashed the party in the third round. His 69 thrust him into the lead, one stroke ahead of Irwin and two ahead of Palmer. Watson, playing with Irwin for the last round, gave in to the pressure and shot a 79. Palmer, his putter ice cold, scored a 76. Irwin's biggest worry, beyond the course itself, was Forrest Fezler. Neither golfer distinguished himself down the stretch. Fezler crashed and burned on the eighteenth with a bad drive and a bogey. Irwin, who opened with a 36, bogeyed two of the last four holes, but finished with a 73.

Irwin's winning aggregate for the tournament was an ungainly 287, some seven strokes above par. In all, only seven sub-par rounds were shot by the world's best golfers. The USGA had been vindicated.

AP/Wide World Photos

1 9 7 5

In the Open, one of the long shots occasionally outlasts the favorites and unexpectedly leaves the course mounting the trophy on the hood of his car. That theory explains how Lou Graham, a baseball cap wedged between top hats on the shelf of life, won the 1975 Open at Medinah Course Number Three.

The chalk choices in the fourth round—Jack Nicklaus and the Bear Apparent, Ben Crenshaw—each had their hands on the hardware but lost their grip. "There will be twenty guys leaving here," Nicklaus said afterward, "who'll say, 'If I'd played halfway decently, I would've won.'"

Nicklaus would have been the guest of honor at the award ceremony if he had not strung bogeys on the sixteenth, seventeenth, and eighteenth holes. Crenshaw could have overtaken Graham and John Mahaffey with two pars, two average scores, at the seventeenth and eighteenth holes. But Crenshaw's approach shot to the seventeenth was weak, and worse, wound up wet. He made five at the par-three and shared third place at 288 with Hale Irwin, Bob Murphy, and Frank Beard, who had been the leader through the first three rounds. Beard shot 78 when 75 would have been his lucky number.

Fishermen like Graham usually lament the one that got away. He had hooked only two minor titles in eleven years of professional golf, so he did not expect to be casting for the Open championship. Graham, thirty-seven then, did not possess the jutting confidence of most champions. "Informal folk from Tennessee" describes him well. His hobbies were fishing and shooting pool and par. He shot an ugly 73 to tie Mahaffey at 287 in the final round, then outshot Mahaffey 71 to 73 in a playoff plainer than calico.

His acceptance speech reflected his humility and surprise at the outcome. "Right now it's hard for me to get in my mind that I won the U.S. Open," he told an audience holding pens, pads, and camera tackle. "I can't imagine it. I don't feel like a U.S. Open champion." Understandable. Simple men who wear the same old shirt throughout the tournament, removing it only to rinse it out every evening, seldom swap their cap for a crown.

UPI/Bettmann

ATLANTA COUNTRY CLUB
DULUTH · GEORGIA

Sometimes one shot among thousands defines an Open, writes a page of golf history, and leaves spectators with an invaluable souvenir. The second shot Jerry Pate struck at the eighteenth hole of the Atlanta Country Club in 1976 belongs on the same page of Open annals with the approach shot Bobby Jones smote at the eighteenth hole of Inwood Country Club to ensure his victory in the 1923 Open, and the second shot Ben Hogan launched at Merion twenty-seven years later that put him in a playoff against Lloyd Mangrum and George Fazio and put him on the scent of his second title.

This rough-to-riches story really began in the fourth round, with Pate standing in clumps of thick Bermuda grass discussing shot options with his caddie, John Considine. His lead— one stroke over Tom Weiskopf and Al Geiberger—was thinner than the green 190 yards ahead of him, but his lie was manageable. The ball lay comfortably on a bed of rough. He said to Considine, "I've got to go for it. This is my one big chance to win the Open."

Although twenty-two years old then, Pate spoke like an antique golfer, an old-timer approaching the seventy-second hole of his career and unexpectedly courting the fickle Open. He confidently chose a five-iron from his bag of weapons. "I felt sure I could make the shot," he said. "I was all pumped up." He stood over the shot and history, swung fluidly, and squarely struck the ball and paydirt. The ball, as though being drawn to the flag by an invisible magnetic impulse, stopped two feet before the cup and rolled on into posterity.

"I knew then I had won the Open," he said. Tap. Birdie. Victory. The heroic three gave Pate 68 for 277, two shots better than Weiskopf and Geiberger and three better than John Mahaffey. Mahaffey, second in 1975 and third in 1976, kept sliding at the end, finishing bogey, bogey, bogey.

"I really wanted to win the Open," Pate said afterward. "I knew I wanted to win as much as those other guys." The Open continually taunts and dares its opponents, luring them to disaster or distinction.

1 9 7 7

Death threats follow more gangsters than golfers to work. In 1977 a mysterious death threat was one more obstruction for Hubie Green to overcome on the obstacle course leading to the Open title. "It's a shame that had to happen," Green said afterward. "I don't believe it bothered me. It was out of my hands. There was nothing I could do."

Fussy golfers like Green—a twitcher, peeker, and fretter on the greens—often crack when the Open pressure valve ruptures, spraying the field with uncertainty. Luckily, he ran out of holes before he ran out of ways to lose the championship. "I choked, but we all choke in the majors," Honest Hubie said after bogeying the seventy-second hole, shooting 70 in the fourth round, 278 overall, and wobbling to victory against Lou Graham, the 1975 Open champion.

Green did not look like someone in need of the Heimlich maneuver when he drove at the eighteenth hole. He swung freely and routinely, and his tee ball came down in the middle of the fairway. In this game, though, the golfer and the golf ball often miscommunicate. The confused ball does not understand body English, and when the golfer aims for the right, the ball frequently flies to the left. Green told himself to avoid the fairway trap on the left, but his ball did not hear the instructions. The insolent ball next flew weakly from the bunker, landing forty feet behind the cup. "I could hear everybody laugh," Green said. 'Well, looks like there's going to be a playoff.'"

Avoiding overtime meant Green had to sink what he thought was an unsinkable second putt. "I had a four-footer, uphill and straight," he said. "That's the hardest putt for me, because I can't hit it straight." He struck the putt gloomily, but the impudent ball finally went to its place at the bottom of the cup.

OPPOSITE PAGE: *Jerry Pate's memorable second shot at the eighteenth hole in the fourth round of the 1976 Open sealed his victory. Hubert Green* (RIGHT) *had to overcome the typical obstacles and an anonymous death threat to win the 1977 Open.*

1 9 7 8

CHERRY HILLS COUNTRY CLUB
DENVER · COLORADO

The field of contenders for the Open trophy always includes members of the rabble—commoners who occasionally sneak into the kingdom and filch the prize from the favorite knights.

Anonymous Andy North won this Open and spent years afterward apologizing for finishing ahead of the field. Nobody but North thought he had an opportunity to defeat the pantheon of par: Jack Nicklaus, Tom Watson, Lee Trevino, Hale Irwin, and Gary Player. "I really did expect to win," North says now. He has to speak boldly; golfers without confidence have less chance of succeeding than of sinking a putt from 35 feet with a sand wedge.

North cites his second-place finish at the Kemper tournament not long before the Open as proof of his potential, but being in the vicinity of victory rarely identifies future Open champions. Open titlists usually possess bucketsful of victories, muscular reputations, and recognizable names and faces. Spectators at the time mistook North for Andy Bean or Jerry Heard, another good, but faceless, golfer. North had won the Westchester Classic in 1977, but people rarely remember the champions of regular tournaments past Sunday evening.

Successive 70s kept North in the headlines and the hunt at Cherry Hills, one long weed because of the thickness of the rough. In the third round he made birdie at the eighteenth hole, shot 71, and led Player by one shot. "I thrive on pressure," says North, who as a child in Wisconsin lived for the change of seasons: football, to basketball, to baseball. "In high school," he goes on, "I was the kind of guy who wanted the ball at the end of the game—in basketball or any sport. I always took that same mentality into golf."

North thought he was retrieving the game ball of sorts from the cup at the thirteenth hole when he sank a birdie putt from eighteen feet. "Beforehand," he says, "I told my caddie [Gary Crandall], 'If I sink this it's over.'" Although his lead grew to five shots, the tournament did not end at the sixty-seventh hole. Suddenly the wind and the pressure were in the gallery following him. He made bogey at the fourteenth hole, double bogey

at the fifteenth, and bogey at the sixteenth. His lead over Dave Stockton and J. C. Snead shrank to one stroke.

North made par at the seventeenth hole and confidently struck his tee ball at the finishing hole. One good approach shot, not Stockton or Snead, stood between North and the title. When his second shot came down in one of the traps guarding the green, his victory was in question. "[Now] you're a little concerned," he later noted. "But to me that was easier than going thirty or forty feet past the hole."

He left the sand shot three feet short and rejoiced. "That's what I wanted," he says, "a makeable putt—uphill and straight—to win the Open."

When he stood over the ball, the wind began snorting. Since sinking putts is difficult enough in breathless conditions, North waited, and waited, and waited. The Open tests players' courage and composure; the Open is a stress test. When the wind finally gave in, North struck the putt into the rear of the cup. "Mental capacity—that's absolutely the essence of what we're talking about here," he says. "You learn to hang in there, you learn to win." North went to the press room dragging a 74 for a total of 285 behind him. He lost to par by one shot, but he beat Stockton and Snead and the odds.

1 9 7 9

INVERNESS CLUB
TOLEDO · OHIO

In 1979, Hale Irwin won his second Open, becoming the fourteenth golfer to win the title more than once. The memorable roots of this championship, however, extend from what has been dubbed the "Hinkle Tree," a spindly spruce twenty-four feet high and sixteen feet wide at its base that the USGA planted alongside the eighth tee before the second round to block the golfers' shortcut to the long par-five.

In the first round Lon Hinkle and others easily and deliberately struck their tee shots onto the seventeenth fairway, shrinking the parallel hole, the eighth, by approximately sixty yards. The timber did not deter golfers from bending balls around the tree or the rigid principles of golf. The Hinkle Tree did not deter-

AP/Wide World Photos

Andy North won the Open in 1978, then spent years afterward practically apologizing for the accomplishment.

mine the outcome of the championship, either, although Tom Purtzer was sniffing at the lead until he took the devil's path and made seven at the eighth hole in the fourth round.

The critical hole of this tournament was the thirteenth, another par-five. Tom Weiskopf made eagle there ahead of Irwin in the third round. "Bang! You're dead," was the symbolic message of the shot. It did not intimidate Irwin, however, who thought himself bulletproof at the time. He matched that three on the same hole with his own aggressive rifle shot from 225 yards. Eagle was a formality from two feet.

Irwin did not look like he would join the small club of multiple Open champions when he shot 74 in the first round, but he went around in 68 in the second round, and a 67 in the third round capped his comeback. Irwin led Weiskopf by three shots at the end of fifty-four holes, and Jerry Pate and Gary Player by six shots with five holes remaining.

Compliant greenskeepers, following USGA orders, modify the diets of Open courses during championship week, depriving the hungry, thirsty grass of nutrients and water in order to toughen the conditions. So, gluttonous Open courses devour whatever nutrient is available, especially leads.

Four helpings of lead were enough to satisfy Inverness, so Irwin had enough of an edge at the end to double bogey the seventeenth hole, bogey the eighteenth, stitch together a 75, and still defeat Pate and Player, former Open champions themselves, by two shots with 284.

"I started choking on the first tee," Irwin said afterward. "This was not your casual round of Sunday golf, an interclub tournament.

"If the pressure doesn't affect you, you're not human."

Professional golfers are pain addicts and the Open title is one of the few anesthetics.

1 9 8 0

BALTUSROL GOLF CLUB
SPRINGFIELD · NEW JERSEY

Golf, more than any other professional sport, permits spectators to march the timeline with their favorite figures, figuratively following them from puberty to Social Security (assisted by the success of the PGA Senior Tour).

America began walking with Jack Nicklaus in 1960, when, as an amateur, he almost won the U.S. Open at Cherry Hills at the age of twenty. In 1980, the world wondered whether Nicklaus had reached the clubhouse of his career. He came to malevolent Baltusrol at forty like an aging movie idol, occasionally resembling his old self when the lighting was obliging and his makeup was flawless. He came to Baltusrol squeezing memories because, when he did, he felt young, aggressive, unbeatable. However, the leap of faith had become for Nicklaus a Grand Canyon broad jump. Father Time caddied his bag now.

Not even legendary golfers possess evergreen games—their swings and nerves gradually grow brown and wizen like those of mortal golfers.

Before this Open, Nicklaus had thought about retiring, about quitting "this silly game." He did not want to embarrass himself or the sport. Winless in two years, he feared degenerating into the golfing equivalent of one of those cemetery fighters who are shamelessly paired with a young boxer on the way up or an older marquee boxer on the way down.

AP/Wide World Photos

AP/Wide World Photos

Nicklaus was not that washed up, but he was an aging athlete motivated in 1980 by a running meter. He had been playing for a living since 1962, and scooping paydirt with both hands all that time. But victories always meant more than money to Emperor Nicklaus, ruler of a $300 million golf and business empire. A fourth Open trophy definitely would be more valuable to him than the paycheck, since Nicklaus knew he was playing the back nine of his career.

Nothing in sports thrills one more than watching the Golden Bear fix that Golden Glare on an improbable feat and then succeed in performing it. Partial success—finishing second, third, or fourth—was not going to fulfill him at Baltusrol; so together with Tom Weiskopf, an old Ohio friend and rival, Nicklaus led an assault on par in the first round.

He and Weiskopf each shot 63, matching the lowest score in Open history. Because Nicklaus perceives rounds of golf as expeditions for perfection, he left the eighteenth green feeling let down after missing a birdie putt from three feet. "I really wanted that 62 and I thought I had it," he said in the press tent.

When Nicklaus began with two wild tee shots, and was one over par after two holes in the second round, even Jeane Dixon could not have predicted what followed: eight birdies and six near-misses. "The last time I putted this well," he said, "might have been the last time I was here [in 1967, when Nicklaus won the Open with a total of 275]."

He shot good Open golf in the second and third rounds, 71 and 70 respectively. For forty-five holes, Nicklaus had been in a time machine, surprising everyone with his record round and his determination that no putt was too long to sink. Then the fangs of Open pressure punctured him and he merely shared the lead with Isao Aoki, the Jack Nicklaus of Japan, whose lucky number had been 68 throughout the first three rounds.

Nicklaus fought rough off the tees and lost two strokes on the incoming six holes, the easiest stretch on the course. His total score, 204, set an Open record but did not comfort him. Nicklaus beat at himself in the press room, unable to accept bogeys at the fourteenth and fifteenth holes and par at the eighteenth. "I'd love to have made this a very dull tournament," he said. "But, instead, I gave back all the lead I had. Right now I'm vulnerable to six, seven, eight players. At ten under, I would've been vulnerable to one or two."

In the fourth round, some Nicklaus nuts hung out of trees on Mountain Avenue to watch their sovereign battle Aoki, the rest of the field, and himself. In golf, doubt can often be more difficult to defeat than par, and Nicklaus spent the first nine holes wondering whether he had enough of that Old Jack Magic on Sunday to finish what he had begun on Thursday. With a bang, bang, birdie, birdie finale, Nicklaus shot 68 in the fourth round and 272 overall. He had flattened Baltusrol like an old tube of toothpaste.

Hale Irwin (OPPOSITE PAGE), *who eleven years later became the oldest champion in Open history, became another multiple Open winner with his victory in 1979. In 1980, Jack Nicklaus* (ABOVE LEFT) *found some of that Old Jack Magic at Baltusrol Country Club, where he had won another Open ten years earlier.*

Aoki did his best to keep up with the record pace Nicklaus set, and indeed would have won any other Open with his total of 274. His only rewards, though, were heaps of cash, second place, and "the greatest lesson of playing with the greatest golfer in history."

Nicklaus did not react to his victory immediately at the trophy ceremony. He stood alone for almost one minute gazing at the rural vista, gratefully scanning the idolatrous gallery and quietly celebrating his resurrection.

Professional athletes die twice, the first time in their middle or late thirties, when nature strips them of youthful ability. While Nicklaus had lost some of his past skills, he had not lost his competitiveness or resolve, often the most powerful weapons in anyone's bag.

1 9 8 1

MERION GOLF CLUB
ARDMORE · PENNSYLVANIA

Golf tests the mind more than the muscles, highlighting its followers' psychological assets and liabilities in neon yellow ink. In this game losers usually defeat themselves with untimely spasms of anger or fear. The final round of the U.S. Open tests the skill, judgment, and composure of the men in and near the lead. George Burns plainly understood the mystery and misery of this addictive mind game at the end of the 1981 Open. He lost his poise and the prize in the fourth round.

Burns had shot three successive rounds in the 60s (69, 66, and 68) at Merion and led the tournament with the lowest score through fifty-four holes in Open history, 203. He was in position to lap the field and tie, splinter, or shatter Jack Nicklaus' record total of 272. His unfortunate feud with Harry Easterly of the USGA probably did Burns in more than the impressive round David Graham shot to win the title.

Burns and the USGA had fought before, beginning in 1975. This incident began when Burns, wound tighter than most golf balls throughout his career, overheard the end of an Easterly remark at the third hole, where Burns had run his long approach putt four feet past the cup. "As I was coming off the

The golfing gods occasionally reward patient, stoic champions. In 1981, such was the case for David Graham (ABOVE). *Tom Watson* (OPPOSITE PAGE) *finally joined the golfing elite with his surprise victory at the 1982 U.S. Open.*

green," Burns recalls, "I heard Harry say, 'that was a terrible first putt but the second one was good.'"

Burns' emotional steampipe burst and he told Easterly, "You've always been a ----head and you still are."

Although there were fifteen holes remaining, Burns, still one shot ahead of Graham, essentially lost the tournament before reaching the fourth tee. "After that," Burns said, "I wasn't the same. I told him what I felt, and let it affect me. I'm the idiot for letting it affect me." The USGA later made its own statement, asserting Burns had misunderstood the private exchange between Easterly and Arthur Rice, the USGA observer for the pairing. His patience and concentration irretrievably lost, Burns lost the lead forever with an angry bogey at

the tenth hole, the shortest and easiest par-four on the course. He wound up shooting 73 and fell from first to second, tied with Bill Rogers. Graham, an Australian whom critics first thought would be a better clubmaker than shotmaker, overtook Burns with an instructive 67, an illuminated illustration of the power of patience and control.

In his best years of professional golf, Graham, whose 273 total was one shot off the Open record, spent more time perfecting his mental approach to the game than the mechanics of the mystifying repetitive swing. "It's the way I learned to play," he said. "On the Australian Tour, if you didn't win, you didn't earn any money....So you learned very quickly how to concentrate...all the time."

1 9 8 2

Although his credentials were impeccable, Tom Watson was just another good golfer until his chip came in at misty, mythological Pebble Beach.

Watson had won the Masters in 1977 and 1981; the British Open in 1975, 1977, and 1980; and more than $2 million over the years. Still, he was not in Jack Nicklaus' class or at his level of fame until Watson sank an impossible chip shot and won his first Open with Nicklaus chasing history. "Every golfer wants to win a major tournament," Watson said, "and the biggest of all is the Open."

Nicklaus was in the scorers' tent accepting congratulations for his record fifth Open title and eighteenth major professional championship when Watson was in trouble on the seventeenth hole, a perilous par-three. His ball was nearly invisible, embedded in deep emerald rough bisecting two bunkers to the left of the cup. Watson was sharing first with Nicklaus, but, in his position, four was a more likely score than two or even three.

"Even if you had a good lie," Nicklaus thought, "you couldn't drop the ball straight down out of your hand on that green and prevent it from going less than ten feet past the pin.

"I figured, 'There's no way in the world he can get it up and down from there [for par].'"

He was correct. Watson did not need two shots to complete the hole—one was enough. "I practiced that shot for hours and hours," he said afterward. "It was the greatest shot of my life, certainly the most meaningful."

With one flick of his magical wedge, he turned bogey into birdie. "I told my caddy, 'I'm not going to try to get it close. I'm going to sink it.' As soon as it landed on the green, I knew it was in. When it went into the hole, I about jumped into the Pacific Ocean."

Watson sank the delicate grass explosion from seventeen feet, then thrust his arms into the air, his putter needlessly in hand, and did a short victory lap around the edge of the green. Then he spun, and, pointing at his caddie, jubilantly yelled, "Told ya!"

The planet did a double take over the surprise ending to the tournament, one of the most exhilarating Opens in history. "It was an incredible shot," Bill Rogers was saying afterward. He had begun the fourth round in first place with Watson. "You could let someone, anyone, hit a hundred balls from there, and they wouldn't hole one."

Watson had lost the Open at Pebble Beach before—in both practice rounds and his mind. "When I was younger, I'd drive down here from Stanford [University] and tee it up at 7 A.M., when I'd have the course to myself. Honestly, I did fantasize about coming down the stretch head to head with Jack Nicklaus in the U.S. Open.

"I'd set to the last couple of holes and say, 'You've got to play these one under par to win the Open.' Of course, I'd always play 'em two over. Then I'd say, 'You've got a long way to go, kid.'"

Under clamping pressure and championship conditions, Watson did not fail. He sank a stylish, but meaningless, birdie putt from eighteen feet at the eighteenth hole, shot 70, and won the tournament by two strokes 282 to 284.

Nicklaus lost to a champion, so there was no dishonor in that, just disappointment. "When he makes that [shot at 17]," Nicklaus said, "the golf tournament's history. I've had it happen before, but I didn't think it was going to happen again. But it did.

"How would I evaluate that shot? One of the worst that ever happened to me. Right up there with Trevino's [chip-in] at Muirfield [on the seventy-first hole of the 1972 British Open]".

An improbable victory did not open the Open sluice for Watson, though he came close to tying Scott Simpson for the title at the Olympic Club in 1987. In the end, Watson may not win another Open, but in 1982 he won his Open. He got the trophy, and golf posterity got one of the greatest shots in golf history.

OPPOSITE PAGE: *Larry Nelson, an elder in the parish of professional golf who taught himself to play the fiendish game by reading a book by Ben Hogan, was the 1983 Open champion. His aggregate score of 132 over the final 36 holes broke the record, set by Gene Sarazen in 1932, by four strokes.*

1 9 8 3

OAKMONT COUNTRY CLUB
OAKMONT · PENNSYLVANIA

The unpredictable golfing gods sometimes bestow the Open title on one of the laity—in this instance Larry Nelson, an elder in the parish of professional golfers.

Although he already had won a major tournament, the 1981 PGA Championship, Nelson did not seem to belong above Tom Watson on the leaderboard of the 1983 Open.

AP/Wide World Photos

In the end, when he sank a serpent of a birdie putt on the seventieth hole and set an Open record of 132 in the final two rounds, there was no place to put his name but first, completing his recovery from the rear. He had been closer to missing the cut than to first halfway through the tournament. He was in twenty-fifth place at the end of thirty-six holes—the equivalent of the back of the bar, where the thirstiest customers usually languish, dehydrate, and evaporate.

Nelson, a quiet man of God who taught himself the devil's game when he came back from Vietnam at the age of twenty-two, did not dissolve in the third round. He shot 65. The lowest round of the tournament put him in second place with Calvin Peete at 213 and one shot behind the leaders, Tom Watson and Seve Ballesteros. The "experts" of the press were too busy predicting and anticipating an intoxicating duel between Watson and Ballesteros to notice Nelson.

In the final round Watson went out in 31, ejecting Ballesteros, at 36, from the lead horse. Nelson countered with 33 on the first nine, but fell three strokes behind. Watson lost two shots of his lead with bogeys at the tenth and twelfth holes, and the third when Nelson struck his second shot one foot from the cup at the fourteenth hole and sank the simple birdie putt. The USGA suspended, then postponed, the round when a thunderstorm submerged the course beneath several inches of rainwater.

All in attendance were thunderstruck Monday morning when Nelson, who closed with a 67 for 280, sank an improbable putt from sixty feet below the cup at the sixteenth hole, a petrifying par-three. When Watson bogeyed the fourteenth hole, Nelson, suddenly hanging on the lip of reality, led by two shots. He made par at the seventeenth hole and bogeyed the eighteenth, but Nelson won the tournament by one stroke anyway, after Watson made three mistakes at two holes, two more than is permissible on any day.

Golf continually seduces, then severs, the soul of the immodest masochist foolish enough to challenge its supremacy. While eternally cruel, golf does occasionally reward persistent, humble pluggers, the unobstrusive servants of the game who possess the stamina and forbearance necessary to follow their dreams and not curse the damn ball when it lands in the damn trees.

AP/Wide World Photos

1 9 8 4

WINGED FOOT GOLF CLUB
MAMARONECK · NEW YORK

In 1984, Greg Norman and Fuzzy Zoeller posed for the sort of mental snapshots that differentiate the Open from the countless corporate classics that fill the golf calendar. It is a war photo of sorts.

Norman sank "the putt heard 'round the world" from forty feet away at the seventy-second hole to tie Zoeller for the lead. Zoeller, thinking he had lost the tournament, jovially waved a white towel in mock surrender while leaning against his golf bag on the left side of the eighteenth fairway. Click, click, click. Get the picture?

Some keepers of the game contend that only gentlemen golf, but rarely does an ambitious professional athlete, competing in the most important tournament of the season, act with such dignity, spontaneity, and sportsmanship. After all, most other sporting gods would have reacted to a devastating body blow such as Norman's incredible putt with a sneer, a growl, a deluge of expletives, and perhaps even a display of physical violence. Zoeller was not rude and he did not brood; everyone was his friend at the 1984 Open, including his opponents.

"Nice shot, partner," Zoeller sincerely told Hale Irwin on numerous occasions when the two of them were skirmishing during the third and fourth rounds. Because Zoeller prefers whistling and grinning to cussing and scowling, he and Irwin were as different as comedian and straight man throughout the tournament. Irwin did plenty of grumbling that year, and not all of it was about the unfortunate 79 he scored in the fourth round, which dropped him from first to sixth place with a total of 284.

"If someone had told me beforehand that I would shoot 79, I would've laughed. I guess the joke's on me. I just don't believe how noisy the gallery was," says Irwin. "Don't get me wrong. I'm not blaming them. It was a fair fight. But I don't

Fuzzy Zoeller displayed uncommon composure and humor at the 1984 Open, a championship competition that was distinguished by a particularly rowdy gallery.

think I've ever stepped away from so many shots as I have the past two days."

Spectators at professional golf tournaments generally act like churchgoers—they stand silently and reverently behind the ropes that separate the real world from the sports world so as not to disturb the high priests of par, some of whom will glare at rambunctious gallery members. These angry looks are generally all that is required to silence the gallery. The unusually loud crowds in 1984 were simply appreciative of Zoeller and Norman, the headliners of a spectacular event that was marked by both drama and humanity.

Norman was closer to the bursting grandstands than he was to the cup when he sank the impossible putt at the eighteenth hole. "I aimed at a spot about twelve feet right of the hole—a brown patch," said Norman, who made miraculous pars at each of the three finishing holes. "When the ball went over it, I knew that it was in the hole."

Despite having lost a lead of four strokes in the fourth round, Zoeller had lost none of his sense of humor. Before the playoff on Monday morning, he gave Norman a cordless phone and the opportunity to call for help. Norman, who plays golf with the commando mentality of a middle linebacker and the carefree, roguish disposition of an old-time riverboat gambler, laughed. He should have accepted the offer and dialed 911, the emergency number.

Norman inexplicably spent three hours either in trouble or in the rough. He made double bogey at the second hole and bogeys at the third and fourth holes, shot 75 overall, and lost the most lopsided playoff in Open history. He lost by eight strokes to Zoeller, whose total of 67 was the lowest playoff score in Open annals. After the playoff, drinks were on Zoeller: he bought fifteen bottles of champagne for the press.

Zoeller's lively personality works in several gears; he downshifts naturally from the humorous to the serious without losing any of his personable "y'all" style. His victory speech was deferential and sentimental. "This is something that's gonna take a period of years to sink in. Wherever I go I'm known as Masters champion Fuzzy Zoeller. Now I'll be known as Masters *and* U.S. Open champion."

The 1984 Opens continues to embody cheerful sports competition and definitely belongs in the U.S. Open photo album.

1 9 8 5

OAKLAND HILLS COUNTRY CLUB
BIRMINGHAM · MICHIGAN

It was the afternoon before the U.S. Open, and Andy North found himself flipping through the tournament program. The name Ralph Guldahl caught his eye. Guldahl, it turned out, had won the 1937 U.S. Open at Oakland Hills. North read the next entry and his eyes widened. Guldahl had also won the following U.S. Open, the 1938 championship at Cherry Hills. Now, this was interesting. North, you see, had won the 1978 Open at Cherry Hills. And here he was, preparing for the difficult Oakland Hills course. "It was really weird," North remembers. "I thought to myself, 'I'm destined to win this tournament. Shoot, I'm going to win this one.'"

There weren't many golfers in the field who would have taken the long odds against North's chances. Indeed, he had won at Cherry Hills seven years earlier, but it had been only his second tour victory ever. Now, thirteen seasons into his career, North still had only those two wins to his credit. Since the U.S. Open win, North had come to be considered something of a fluke. Injuries, particularly bone spurs in his elbow, vastly diminished North's game. The six-foot-four-inch, 200-pound golfer fell to 98th on the money list in 1983 and plummeted to 149th in 1984, with a paltry $22,131 in winnings. North had kept the faith. Once he was healthy again, he rebuilt his swing. He was among the top ten at the Hawaiian Open, but missed the cut at Westchester before traveling early to Oakland Hills. His practice rounds were superb; North felt better than he had in years.

His first round of 70 was modest enough, but he blistered the course in the second round with a 65 that featured five birdies and no bogeys. But North was almost an afterthought in the wake of Taiwan's T. C. Chen. Playing in the U.S. Open for the first time, Chen put together rounds of 65 and 69 to match the thirty-six-hole record and take a one-stroke lead over North. Those low scores were deceptive, because some of golf's greatest names didn't even make the cut. Lee Trevino, scoring 76 and 72 for a 148, Tom Watson, with 75 and 72 for a 147, and Ben Crenshaw, who shot 78 and 72 to total 150, were all finished after two rounds.

Saturday was a wet, chilly, raw day. Chen, 69, and North, 70, maintained their positions, and most of the rest of the field backed up. North wasn't discouraged to be two strokes off the lead. "It was the kind of day you win an Open by playing a solid round," North says. "I didn't eliminate myself." The press, meanwhile, was giving North a hard time. "Since 1978 was a fluke," they asked, "do you really expect to win?"

North was paired with Chen on Sunday and, at least early on, it seemed as though Chen was the future U.S. Open champion. When he birdied the second hole after North bogeyed the first, his lead was four strokes. On the fifth hole, Chen lost the tournament. His second shot on the par-four hole flew into the trees and settled deep in the rough. Instead of playing it safe, Chen tried to play a pitch-and-run to the hole. His third shot fell short of the green and back into the rough. When it was all over, Chen had taken eight strokes, while North escaped with a clean par. The championship was even.

It was clear from the beginning that North wasn't playing well. He couldn't keep his drives in the fairways and his putter wasn't especially sharp. It was Chen's failure under pressure, however, that kept him in it. Chen three-putted the sixth hole, then bogeyed the seventh and eighth. North's lead was now three shots, but he promptly self-destructed, bogeying the ninth, tenth, and eleventh holes. Dave Barr began to close on

North and actually led the tournament at one point. Down the stretch, though, Barr, too, failed. He bogeyed the final two holes to join Denis Watson in the clubhouse at 280.

North knew the Open hung in the balance as he eyed his precarious position in the bunker near the seventeenth green. He was twenty feet from the cup, but he couldn't even see it from the sand. North blasted to within inches of the hole and made a spectacular par. That preserved his one-stroke lead, and when Barr bogeyed the final hole it was a two-stroke advantage. Playing it safe, North bogeyed the eighteenth to finish with a 74 and an aggregate of 279, one better than Barr, Watson, and Chen. North finished one-under-par, the first golfer in five national championships at Oakland Hills to produce a red number. No one in the press corps mentioned anything about flukes after North's triumph.

Small wonder, for North had become only the fifteenth golfer in history to win two U.S. Opens. "I hope history is kinder to me than it was in June of 1985," North later said. "I've had a number of guys come up to me in recent years to talk about it. Billy Ray Brown, after he had a chance at Medinah [in 1990], said, 'Man, I could barely function out there. I couldn't control myself. And you won the thing twice.' When a guy who is your peer understands what it takes to win the Open, well, that's great."

1 9 8 6

SHINNECOCK HILLS GOLF CLUB
SOUTHAMPTON · NEW YORK

Ninety years earlier, Scotsman Jim Foulis had won the second U.S. Open with a 78 and 74 for a 152 on the painfully young Shinnecock Hills layout. The greens were too small, the bunkers too large, and the effect was that of a British links course. When the world's best professionals arrived in Southampton in 1986, they found the same crafty circuit.

On Thursday the rain and wind were almost unbearable; the average first-round score was somewhat over 75. Only one golfer, stylish Bob Tway, managed to break even by matching par at 70. Australia's Greg Norman was one stroke back. Friday was far kinder, and the scores began to drop. Norman smoked a 69 and led at the midpoint with a total of 140. Lee Trevino, at the age of forty-seven, was three strokes back in second. Ray Floyd, a fixture on the tour, was third after an opening-day 75 and a subsequent 69.

Floyd had never before won the U.S. Open, but his résumé left many wondering why. He had won nineteen tournaments to that point, including three of major status (the PGA title in 1969 and 1982 and the Masters in 1976). Yet his twenty-one previous appearances in the Open had been washouts. Strangely, he had only two top-ten finishes. Floyd, forty-two years old then, had a reputation as a money player. As the tournament wound down and the hole seemed to get smaller and smaller, Floyd usually stepped up taller.

In the third round Norman continued to support the theory that he was one of the game's best players. He shot a nerveless 71, which left him at 211, a shot ahead of Trevino and Hal Sutton. Floyd, who shot a 70, crept a stroke closer. The fourth round was a wild affair. No fewer than nine golfers found themselves tied for the lead at one point late in the afternoon. As Floyd knew, "When you get down to the final nine holes of a U.S. Open, everybody starts making bogeys."

OPPOSITE PAGE: *Ray Floyd parted the masses at Shinnecock Hills Country Club in Southampton, New York, on his way to a dazzling victory in the 1986 U.S. Open.*

On the twelfth hole, it looked like Floyd would follow suit. He was looking at a sticky twenty-foot putt for par, but he stepped up and rolled it in. The younger golfers around him began to wilt. Norman, for instance, bogeyed the ninth hole and stumbled to a finishing round of 75. Sutton took extra strokes on the twelfth and fifteenth holes. Tway, who had the best chance to beat Floyd, made a seven on the sixteenth hole. Floyd sank two modest birdie putts of four feet at the thirteenth hole and ten feet at the sixteenth, and fashioned a powerful 66, including a score of 32 on the back nine. After that opening 75, Floyd had played Shinnecock in 204 shots over the last fifty-four holes, tying an Open record. His final total of 279 made him the only golfer under par for the tournament.

1 9 8 7

OLYMPIC CLUB
SAN FRANCISCO · CALIFORNIA

The U.S. Open favorites were quivering in their spikes as the 1987 U.S. Open unfolded at Olympic. They knew that the marvelous championship course had not been kind to the stars of the past. Someone named Jack Fleck had stunned the great Ben Hogan at the 1955 Open. Billy Casper had come back from a seven-shot deficit to tie Arnold Palmer before beating him in the playoff in 1966. Who would be humbled at this Olympic?

Apparently, it would not be Tom Watson. He was thirty-seven now, and clearly past his prime. He had not won on the tour in three years and it had been five years since he made his miraculous pitch to win the U.S. Open at Pebble Beach. Watson opened the tournament with a fairly pedestrian 72, then blinded the field with a 65 that reminded observers of the days in the late 1970s when he dominated golf. The total of 137, equaled only by Mark Wiebe, placed him three under par. By Sunday, and the last nine glorious holes at Olympic, it had come down to Watson, the six-time PGA Player of the Year, and Scott Simpson. Wiebe, Jack Nicklaus, Seve Ballesteros, Ben Crenshaw, and Curtis Strange had all fallen back.

Playing in the pair ahead of Watson, Simpson birdied the fourteenth hole to tie Watson for the lead at one under par.

Simpson was something of a curiosity. Playing at the University of Southern California, he had been the NCAA champion in 1976 and 1977. He joined the tour in 1979, and though he was a steady money earner, Simpson had won only three tournaments, one of them earlier in the season, the Greater Greensboro Open. Still, Simpson was a terrific putter and had long, clean irons. Simpson dropped a thirty-foot putt on the fifteenth to take a one-stroke lead over Watson. Within seconds, Watson spun in a birdie of his own on the fourteenth hole to tie it again. Simpson came back with his third consecutive birdie putt, a fifteen-footer on the sixteenth hole.

Looking at the leaderboard for the first time, Simpson saw his name a stroke ahead of Watson. His second shot on seventeen found the bunker, but Simpson did not quail. Rather, he reminded himself that two other golfers had been in his shoes. "I thought about Fleck and Casper," Simpson says. "The one thing I knew I had going for me was that I knew the veterans had lost two times before here. If Jack Fleck could come from behind and win, then I could do it, too."

It wasn't easy. Simpson exploded from the trap and knocked down a seven-foot putt for par. His par at the eighteenth hole was routine. Now it was left for Watson to show

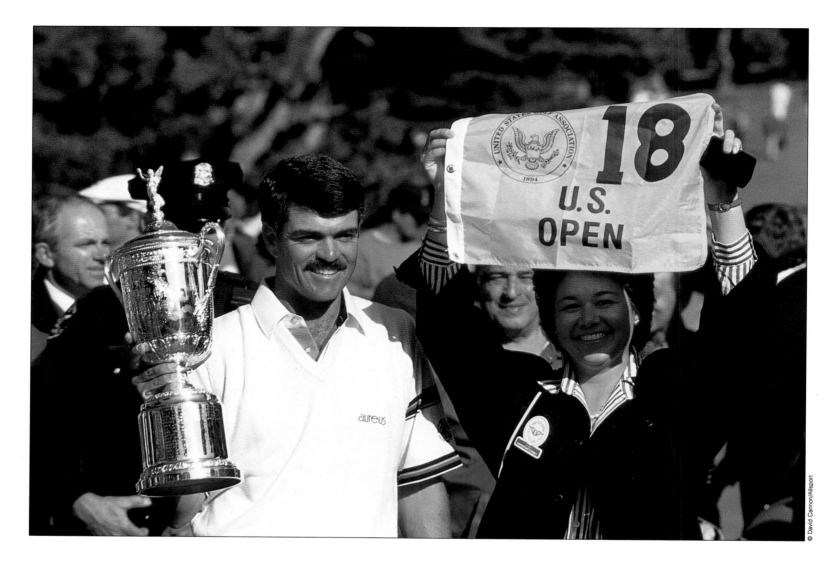

© David Cannon/Allsport

his championship mettle and birdie the seventy-second hole. Watson's pitch to the green was disastrously short and he was faced with a forty-five-foot putt to tie. Watson gave it a tremendous try, but the ball stopped inches short of the hole. Simpson, with a little help from history and Olympic, had produced another upset.

1	9	8	8

THE COUNTRY CLUB
BROOKLINE · MASSACHUSETTS

In 1988, the U.S. Open came back to The Country Club, the scene of Francis Ouimet's legendary victory over Englishmen Harry Vardon and Ted Ray seventy-five years earlier. Fifty years later, Julius Boros beat Arnold Palmer in another classic championship in Brookline, Massachusetts. Two U.S. Open tournaments, two playoffs. Could the 1988 version be any different?

Mike Nicolette, Bob Gilder, and Masters champion Sandy Lyle all shot 68 in the opening round to tie for the lead. Defending Open champion Scott Simpson emerged as the thirty-six-hole leader, having shot 69 and 66 for a commanding 135. Larry Mize was one stroke back. It wasn't until Sunday, however, that the tournament was reduced to two men: Curtis Strange and England's Nick Faldo.

Strange had won fourteen tournaments in his eleven-year career, sometimes in spectacular fashion. He was the professional tour's leading money winner in 1985 and again in 1987, but he had never won a major championship. At the age of thirty-three, a major was all that was missing from Strange's life. "Well, no, I didn't think about winning a major all the time," Strange says. "To me, it was the next step. I was playing well at the time; I had just come off winning the Memorial and Hale [Irwin] had just called me the best player in the world. I felt if I played the way I had been I had a chance in Brookline."

OPPOSITE PAGE: *Scott Simpson had the look of champion after dispatching golf's marquee names at Olympia Club in 1987. Simpson edged Tom Watson in a memorable duel.*

Faldo, an intense competitor himself, would win the Masters in 1989 and 1990. Strange caught Faldo on the seventh hole of the final round. He birdied the tenth hole to jump into the lead, then Faldo answered with a six-foot putt for birdie on the fifteenth. Both golfers, feeling the pressure, butchered their approaches to the sixteenth green. Strange found the rough and Faldo was in the bunker. Strange managed to hole his twenty-five-foot putt, while Faldo two-putted. "I always kind of felt in control," Strange says. "But that twenty-five-footer really got me excited. There are very few times on the golf course that I show emotion, but that was one of them."

Now Strange had a stroke in hand. It weighed heavily on him, though. Strange made two great shots to the seventeenth green before a twelve-foot birdie putt got away from him. It traveled five feet past the hole. Then he missed that putt for par. "The green at seventeen was a new green and a lot faster than I thought it would be," Strange says. "I was in shock after I missed the putt for par." Faldo made a four and it was even again. Both men parred the eighteenth, and The Country Club had its third playoff in three U.S. Opens. But Strange essentially won the U.S. Open on that eighteenth hole.

Strange remembers: "I tried to regroup from seventeen real quick, but I pulled the shot off the eighteenth tee and found the rough. My second shot left me in the bunker, about thirty-five feet from the hole. I figured, 'If you're going to lose, lose with concentration and doing your best.' That bunker shot on eighteen got me in the playoffs, it was a huge, huge shot. I got it to within eighteen inches of the hole."

Strange, who hadn't slept at all for two nights, struggled through another sleepless night. He won the playoff by wielding a torrid putter. In eighteen holes, Strange needed a single putt on nine greens. The biggest was a thirty-foot putt for birdie on the thirteenth hole. Faldo, meanwhile, three-putted and Strange took a three-stroke lead. Ultimately, Strange's 71 was four strokes better than Faldo's offering of 75.

"This is the greatest thing I've ever done," Strange said afterward. "This is the greatest feeling I've ever had. This means what every little boy dreams about when he's playing golf late in the afternoon by himself with four balls. It means all the work I've done over all the years has paid off. And maybe it means that Curtis Strange will be looked at now in a different way."

After winning the 1988 U.S. Open
at The Country Club, Curtis
Strange knew that his chances
of winning again the following
year were slim; Ben Hogan had
been the last golfer to repeat as
champion, in 1950 and 1951.
In 1989, at Oak Hill, Strange
matched Hogan with a gritty
victory and himself became a part
of history.

1 9 8 9

OAK HILL COUNTRY CLUB
ROCHESTER · NEW YORK

Curtis Strange had played well after winning the U.S. Open a year earlier, but in his private moments he wondered if it had been a fluke. Oak Hill was a chance to prove that he was a golfer for the ages. After all, no one had repeated as the U.S. Open winner since Ben Hogan managed the feat in 1950 and 1951. "I wasn't thinking about defending, about winning," Strange says. "I wanted to be respectable, to do a good job defending. You try not to put too much pressure on yourself. I wasn't playing as well going into Oak Hill as I was the year before. But once you get there, you get more fired up, you do things better."

Oak Hill had been inundated by rain, so the slippery greens were slow and moist. In the first round three golfers, Payne Stewart, Bernhard Langer, and Joe Don Blake, all ripped off four-under-par 66s. In the second round, Strange proved he was no fluke; he shot a searing 64 to take the lead after thirty-six holes. In the third round, Strange proved he was mortal. He shot a disappointing 73 and forced himself to hit practice balls until dusk fell.

"I played very poorly that round," he says. "It wasn't the worst score I should have had. This was my chance of a lifetime and it was getting away. I found a little something on the practice tee. I had been floundering somewhat, missing both ways. I tried to go back and miss it one way, to find a pattern. So I started cutting the ball. It wasn't always the best percentage shot, but it's what I had to do."

Tom Kite, who was in the midst of a hot streak, led the tournament with eighteen holes left to play. Kite was the game's most consistent player at the time and would go on to lead all money winners that year, with earnings of $1,395,278. But could he win a major tournament, the marquee event that had escaped him over a distinguished eighteen-year career? That question had already been answered by Scott Simpson, who had won the Open in 1987. Kite was two strokes ahead of Simpson and three ahead of Strange going into the throat-tightening final eighteen holes.

Strange had been down this road before. He knew that birdies did not win the Open, pars did. While Kite, 78, and Simpson, 75, went backwards with truly dismal rounds, Strange was steady. He opened the last round with fifteen consecutive pars. "It takes a lot of pars to win a U.S. Open," Strange says. "A lot of them. You have to understand what U.S. Opens do to people in the last round. Patience, if you can handle it, is the key. It comes from confidence in your ability. If Tom had played well on the front side, I would have had to be more aggressive. I thought I'd need a 69 or a 70 to have a chance, but when Tom triple-bogeyed at five, he played into my hands. At that point, I was more confident than I'd been the Wednesday coming into the tournament."

Strange's fifteenth par had not come easily; he needed a tricky little seven-footer to keep his streak intact. Then, with a one-stroke lead, he birdied the sixteenth for a two-shot lead. It was, he would say later, the most critical putt of the tournament. Strange parred the seventeenth and then, playing cautiously, bogeyed the eighteenth for an even-par round and a victorious total of 278, matching his winning score the year before at The Country Club. Instructively, Strange was the only golfer among the top six not to play his worst round of the tournament.

By winning back-to-back U.S. Opens, Strange earned a place in golfing history. Only Hogan, Willie Anderson, John McDermott, Bobby Jones, and Ralph Guldahl had ever done it before.

"The Ben Hogan thing was never a big deal to me," Strange says. "To me, it was important because it hadn't been done in a long time. Some of the great players had never done it before, like Nicklaus, Palmer, Trevino, Watson. It wasn't so much doing it, it was them not doing it.

"It's hard to put it in perspective. I mean, I'm in the middle of my career. Later on it will sink in. I'll tell you, though, when people get me going about The Country Club, I still get goosebumps. I think I always will. Oak Hill was more a feeling of accomplishment."

1 9 9 0

MEDINAH COUNTRY CLUB
MEDINAH · ILLINOIS

Since winning the U.S. Open in 1979, his second championship, Hale Irwin had settled into a comfortable career. He won six tournaments over the next six seasons and made good money, his place in history secure. Then for five years, Irwin didn't win anything. He was lucky to be included in the field at Medinah, for his exemptions had run out. He had placed ninety-third on the money list in 1989 and prospects weren't any better for 1990. Aware of his place in the game, particularly in the U.S. Open, the USGA extended a special invitation to Irwin, who had turned forty-five earlier that month.

In truth, Medinah did not play like a classic U.S. Open course. Rain had softened the greens and the wind that usually made the course so treacherous was absent for the opening round. With the rough around the fairways no more than window dressing, no fewer than thirty-nine golfers broke par. Then forty-seven more did it on Friday. Through two rounds, Tim Simpson led Jeff Sluman by a stroke and Mike Donald by two.

Donald, an anonymous professional from Hollywood, Florida, surprised most observers by staying in contention down the stretch. After three rounds, Donald and Billy Ray Brown led Curtis Strange and Larry Nelson by two strokes. Amazingly, twenty-five golfers were bunched within four shots. One of them was Irwin.

After the first nine holes, in which he posted a modest 36, Irwin caught fire. He birdied the eleventh, twelfth, thirteenth, and fourteenth holes to go seven under par for the tournament. At the turn, he had been six shots behind Donald. Now, he was within two. Donald was actually playing quite well, making par after par. On the sixteenth, though, he took his only bogey of the day. With the rest of the field swooning all around him, the chances of winning looked good.

Irwin's last chance was literally a long shot. He trailed Donald by a stroke. He had already missed relatively short putts on the sixteenth and seventeenth holes, perhaps a sign that age had dulled his nerves. Irwin knew he needed a birdie for a share of the lead, so he stroked it boldly and watched as it spun over the gentle hump in the middle of the green, broke in a sweeping curve six feet to the left of the hole, and then twisted back, incredibly, into the cup. It was an impossible shot, and even Irwin could scarcely believe he had holed it. He set off on a joyous dash around the green, slapping hands with the spectators and blowing them kisses. Irwin had come back in 31 for a 67. Predictably, Donald finished the last two holes in par and forced a playoff.

After eighteen holes, it was still even. Donald had lost a two-stroke lead when Irwin birdied the sixteenth hole and Donald bogeyed the eighteenth. Both golfers finished with 74s, and the Open was confronted with its first sudden-death playoff in history. Irwin finished off Donald quickly; he rifled an iron to within eight feet of the first hole and calmly dropped the putt for his third U.S. Open victory.

1 9 9 1

HAZELTINE NATIONAL GOLF CLUB
CHASKA · MINNESOTA

Since the mid-1980s, Payne Stewart had developed a reputation as one of the professional tour's finest golfers. Three times, in 1986, 1989, and 1990, Stewart had been among the season's top three money winners. He had somehow backed that up with only one major victory, the 1989 PGA Championship. Even that win was tainted because Mike Reid had faltered over the last three holes when Stewart was already in the clubhouse. Prospects for a major breakthrough in 1991 didn't look good when Stewart missed ten weeks of competition with a nerve problem in his neck.

Somehow, Stewart had his neck and his game in shape for Hazeltine. He fired a 67 in the first round to tie Nolan Henke for the lead. Stewart followed with a 70 on Friday, good for a one-shot lead over Henke, Corey Pavin, and the omnipresent Scott Simpson. The third round was the toughest of the tournament. Pavin disappeared with a 79, while Stewart and Simpson struggled in with a 73 and a 72, respectively.

That set up a head-to-head battle between Stewart and Simpson on Sunday. They teed off with a six-under-par, four-shot lead over the field, and no other golfer would ever come within three strokes. Simpson, on the strength of two birdies, held a two-stroke advantage when they reached the sixteenth, Hazeltine's toughest hole. Simpson's drive caught the rough and he ultimately bogeyed, while Stewart's birdie putt narrowly missed. With two holes left to play, Simpson's lead was down to a single shot. Simpson's drive was wild again, and he left himself with a daunting fifteen-foot putt for par, which he missed. Stewart also missed a twenty-foot putt for birdie, and the two men were forced to return Monday for an eighteen-hole playoff.

Neither man played particularly well in the extra round, though Stewart fared a shade better than Simpson. It unfolded

much the way Sunday's round had. There was Simpson leading again by two strokes with three holes to play when disaster struck. Again. Stewart recovered nicely from a bad drive and stroked a bold eighteen-foot putt into the cup for a birdie. Simpson, shaken, missed his par putt of four feet, and it was dead even. When Simpson bogeyed the seventeenth, Stewart was in control. His middling 75 was two strokes better than Simpson's 77. Though Stewart's score was the worst to win a playoff since 1927, he was finally, after all the success and unnatural expectations, a golfer of major proportions.

1 9 9 2

For twenty seasons on the PGA Tour, Tom Kite was the model of consistency. The five-foot-eight-inch, 155-pound Texan had won more money than any golfer in history, a staggering $7 million, by the time he reached Pebble Beach in 1992. Though he had won no fewer than fifteen Tour events, there were three tournaments he failed to win and that dogged him at every turn: the 1984 Masters, the 1985 British Open at St. George, and the 1989 U.S. Open at Oak Hill. For all of his glories, the amazing amount of money he had won, six Ryder Cup appearances for the United States, and two Vardon Trophy Awards, Kite was not universally recognized as a great golfer. Something was lacking, and that something was a victory in a major tournament.

Despite the fact that he was one of only six golfers who played all three Opens at Pebble Beach, in 1972, 1982, and 1992, Kite, forty-two when he teed up at Pebble Beach, was not exactly a pre-tournament favorite. The mantle of favorite went to Fred Couples, David Love III, and Mark O'Meara. Thus it was a huge surprise when Gil Morgan, the forty-five-year-old optometrist, quickly disappeared in front of the pack ahead of the field at a docile Pebble Beach, shooting 66 and 69 over the first 36 holes. The wind off the Pacific Ocean had quieted and Morgan made a mockery of the course. He started the third round three shots ahead of the field and made three birdies in the first seven holes to go a ridiculous 12 under par, a figure

Payne Stewart (ABOVE) *finally delivered on the promise of his early career with a breakthrough victory in the 1991 U.S. Open at Hazeltine. He edged Scott Simpson 75 to 77 in the playoff. Tom Kite* (FOLLOWING PAGE), *a perennial second-place finisher for most of his career, was a popular champion in the 1992 Open at Pebble Beach.*

© David Cannon/Allsport

that, if it stood, would shatter the old U.S. Open record. It was certainly good enough for a seven-stroke lead. Then the wind kicked up and Pebble extracted a few pounds of flesh.

Morgan took a double bogey on the eighth hole, a bogey on the ninth, and another double bogey on the tenth along the shores of Carmel Bay. Bogeys on the eleventh and twelfth holes and another double bogey on the fourteenth hole cost him the biggest advantage since Arnold Palmer lost a seven-stroke lead in the final nine holes of the 1966 Open. Morgan rallied after a fashion, scoring birdies with thirty-foot putts on the sixteenth and eighteenth holes, but his lead was down to a single stroke over Ian Woosnam, Mark Brooks, and Kite. Many experts thought that Woosnam, who had won in the crucible of Augusta in 1991, was in the best position to win. But when the wind began gusting past forty miles per hour, the smart money was on Kite, a man who was known to fly as well as his namesake in heavy weather.

Champions in past years had produced memorable shots at the seventeenth hole at Pebble Beach. Jack Nicklaus had driven a rocket of a one-iron off the flagstick to sew up the 1972 title, while Tom Watson's remarkable chip-in beat Nicklaus in 1982.

Kite's precious moment came earlier, on the 107-yard seventh hole. He had pushed a six-iron shot off the elevated tee into the left rough and was hoping to just get close with his sand wedge. The ball flew from the rough, raced across the green, and banked into the hole off the flagstick. When he saved a bogey from a hazard two holes later, Kite began to realize that he was approaching a major accomplishment.

He finished with a steady even-par 72 and an aggregate of 285, a three-under-par score that was two strokes better than Jeff Sluman. Morgan struggled in with an 81 and Woosnam recorded a 79. Only four players finished the final round under par, and only Kite and Sluman finished all four days in the red numbers. In fact, twenty of the sixty-six golfers did not break 80 and the average score was 77.263.

"There have been a lot of opportunities to win big tournaments," Kite said later, savoring his finest moment. "I've let some slip away. And some were taken away from me, not by my own fault but by somebody else's great play.

"At Oak Hill, I was playing very well. I felt it was my tournament to win or lose. And I lost it. I felt the same way here; that it was my tournament to win or lose. And I won it."

© David Cannon/Allsport

1 9 9 3

BALTUSROL GOLF CLUB
SPRINGFIELD · NEW JERSEY

Baltusrol is a challenging 7,152-yard test of championship golf, but the lack of rain in the weeks leading up to the 1993 U.S. Open had left the rough a little thin, and overnight watering before the first round had made the greens soft and inviting. When the 156-man field averaged 72.282 strokes for the first round, more than a stroke under the previous record (set in 1989), the stage was set for history to be made.

The trio of Scott Hoch, Joey Sindelar, and Craig Parry led the charge with a score of 66, which was four under par and three strokes off the tournament's first-round record, set by Jack Nicklaus and Tom Weiskopf the last time the Open was played at Baltusrol, in 1980. Only one stroke behind these players, tied with veteran golfer Craig Stadler, was the unassuming Lee Janzen.

There had been championship flashes before, but Janzen, who was twenty-eight years old in 1993, seemed to lack the confidence and maturity necessary to win golf's biggest prizes. He had led in the Masters after one round in April and then promptly disappeared by shooting 73-76-77 (he finished thirty-ninth). In the three previous U.S. Opens in which he had played, Janzen hadn't made a single cut and had failed to shoot lower than 74. In his favor, it must be noted that he had won the 1993 Phoenix Open and tied for third at the Buick Classic in Westchester a week before the U.S. Open.

Janzen bogeyed the opening hole of the second round, but then rallied, finishing the round with his second consecutive 67. This gave him a two-stroke lead over former champions Payne Stewart and Tom Watson. Janzen's total of 134 tied the thirty-six-hole record set by Nicklaus at Baltusrol in 1980 and by T.C. Chen at Oakland Hills in 1985.

"At the beginning of the year, making the cut here would have been just great," said Janzen. "I didn't try to put too much into being in the lead, so maybe the low-key approach. At the Masters, I got too much into trying to make birdies; I was a little overaggressive and didn't stay patient enough. Today, I felt more confident."

At Baltusrol in 1993, Lee Janzen equaled Lee Trevino's astounding feat of shooting four rounds in the 60s in a single U.S. Open.

After a third-round 69, Janzen clung to a one-stroke lead over Stewart, who was the odds-on favorite to take the championship he had first won in 1991. When Janzen lost the lead at the twelfth hole, it looked like he was wilting again. But he dropped an eighteen-foot putt at the fourteenth hole for a birdie, and on the sixteenth hole lightning struck.

Stewart was already safely on the green, but Janzen, whose five-iron tee shot had landed his ball in the rough in front of the green, found himself thirty feet from the hole. Janzen, remarkably, took a sand wedge and chipped the ball into the hole for a decisive birdie. This was a back-to-the-future stroke reminiscent of Watson's chip-in birdie on the seventeenth hole to beat Jack Nicklaus in the 1982 Open at Pebble Beach. Janzen, whose childhood hero was Watson, made the connection immediately.

"When it went in, I thought about Watson's shot and how I jumped in the air and nearly touched the ceiling twelve feet high because he was always the guy I rooted for. And I thought somehow I was destined to win."

Janzen also birdied the eighteenth hole—his third in the final five—to finish with a 69 for the round and a total of 272, two strokes better than Stewart. Janzen tied the tournament record set by Nicklaus at Baltusrol in 1980 and became only the second man (following Lee Trevino) to shoot four rounds in the 60s in a single Open.

"I never knew if I had it in me to do it," Janzen said. "I gave it my best every step of the way. There are a lot of guys who I feel have better games than I do. For me to come through like this will probably be the overachievement of my life."

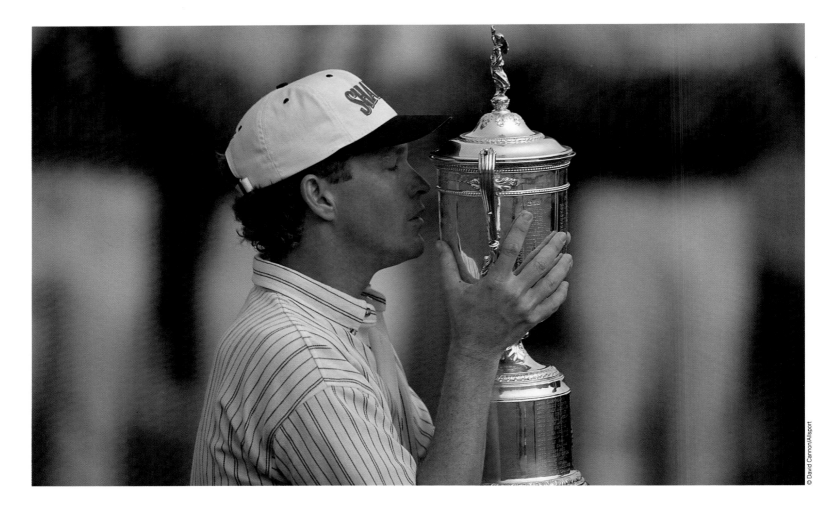

1 9 9 4

OAKMONT COUNTRY CLUB
OAKMONT · PENNSYLVANIA

For five days in June 1994, in the sweltering Pennsylvania heat, the world's best professional golfers fought their way through the great course at Oakmont Country Club. The U.S. Open began with 159 golfers, a number that was culled to sixty-five after the first two rounds. Then, in a history-making third round, three of those golfers—Ernie Els of South Africa, Loren Roberts of the United States, and Colin Montgomerie of Scotland—finished seventy-two holes with identical five-under-par, 279-shot totals. Then, after another grinding eighteen holes at Oakmont in a Monday playoff, it came down to two men—Els and Roberts—who were forced to fight it out in a sudden-death decision. The championship that had opened with such majesty and promise was delivering golf excitement in spades.

The first-round leaderboard was a veritable who's who of golf. The venerable Tom Watson (now forty-four years old), the 1982 champion, beat Oakmont in the sultry ninety-seven-degree heat with a sizzling 68. Fifty-four-year-old Jack Nicklaus, Watson's dueling partner for so many years, was a stroke back, tied with three-time Open champion Hale Irwin, Els, and Frank Nobilo of New Zealand. Ben Chrenshaw, Greg Norman, Bernhard Langer, and Fred Couples were all within four shots of the lead.

In the second round, Montgomerie shot a numbing 65, bringing his total to 136, which was good for a one-stroke lead over Irwin and John Cook. Nicklaus, who shot a steady 70, was tied for third with Jeff Maggert. Two-time champion Curtis Strange, with a pair of 70s, and Watson, with 73 in the second round, were only four and five strokes off the pace, respectively.

The third round belonged to youth. Els, only twenty-four years old in the 1994 Open, proved stronger than the resilient champions of the past. He had finished second the week before at the Buick Classic, just behind 1993 U.S. Open winner Lee Janzen, and his extraordinarily sweet swing led him to a third-round 66, bringing him to a total of 206, two shots better than Nobilo. Watson recovered from his poor showing in the second round to post another score of 68, putting him at the top of a foursome at 209 (the others were Irwin, Montgomerie, and Roberts, who scored the tournament's best for a single round: a sparkling 64).

Not since Australian David Graham had shown enormous patience and prevailed at Merion in 1981 had a foreigner won the U.S. Open. With Els in the lead, the likelihood of this happening again seemed great. If Saturday was the day that laid Oakmont bare, Sunday was the old course's time for revenge. "Someone said that Opens aren't won, they are backed into," observed Roberts after the final scores had been posted. "It was just another classic Open."

But it wasn't over. With Els shooting a nervous 73 and Roberts and Montgomerie scoring matching 70s, Sunday ended with a three-way tie for the lead. In most tournaments, ties are broken with a hole-by-hole, sudden-death battle. In the U.S. Open, it is an 18-hole playoff that has all the tension and excitement of match play. After two holes, it appeared that Els was out of the picture—he bogeyed the first hole and then disappeared with a savage triple-bogey on the par-four second. He birdied the third hole, however, and somehow regained his composure; he was not to be so easily dismissed. With Montgomerie fading gradually out of contention (he finished with a 78), Els slowly reeled in Roberts. Both men birdied the seventeenth hole and came to the eighteenth tied at three over par.

Roberts, one of the Professional Golf Association Tour's best putters, dropped his eight-foot putt for par and Els sank his four-footer to record a 74 and force sudden death. Only one U.S. Open had finished in dramatic sudden death: the 1990 tournament at Medinah Country Club, in which Hale Irwin birdied the first extra hole to defeat Mike Donald.

Els nearly won on the first extra hole, the tenth, but Roberts made a dramatic putt for par. On the eleventh, however, Roberts lost his drive in the deep rough to the right of the fairway, and his second shot landed in the bunker guarding the front of the green. Els, meanwhile, made two clean shots and was looking at an eighteen-foot birdie opportunity. Roberts hit a dreadful shot from the bunker and watched as his ball spun

OPPOSITE PAGE: *Savoring the sweetness of victory: Lee Janzen birdied three of his final five holes to win the 1993 Open by two strokes.*

© Gary Newkirk/Allsport

inexplicably right and stopped some thirty feet from the hole. His fourth shot, a desperation putt for par, actually hit the back of the cup, but its momentum took it around and out. As a result, Els needed only two putts to win. The second, a three-footer, gave him a par on this essential hole and his first win on American soil, making him only the fourth non-American champion since 1928.

"You have to make the shots when they count," said Roberts. "That's what Ernie did."

Said Els, "It's like a dream come true. It started off so badly; we never really played any great golf because we were all a little nervous. But I always wanted to win a major tournament, and I'm still pretty young." And then he paused briefly before adding, "I wouldn't mind doing it again some day."

Twenty-four-year-old Ernie Els battled through sudden death to win at Oakmont in 1994, becoming only the fourth non-American to win the Open since 1928.

A LIST OF CHAMPIONS

The following is a list of the U.S. Open champions over the years, beginning in 1895. Each entry indicates the year, the winner, and the winning score. Entries that have more than one number for the score indicate tournaments that were won in playoff competition. The 1990 Open was won in sudden-death playoff competition over one hole. The 1994 Open required two holes of sudden-death playoff.

Year	Winner	Score	Year	Winner	Score
1895	Horace Rawlins	173	1927	Tommy Armour	301-76
1896	James Foulis	152	1928	Johnny Farrell	294-143
1897	Joe Lloyd	162	1929	Bobby Jones	294-141
1898	Fred Herd	328	1930	Bobby Jones	287
1899	Willie Smith	315	1931	Billy Burke	292-149-148
1900	Harry Vardon	313	1932	Gene Sarazen	286
1901	Willie Anderson	331-85	1933	John Goodman	287
1902	Laurie Auchterlonie	307	1934	Olin Dutra	293
1903	Willie Anderson	307-82	1935	Sam Parks	299
1904	Willie Anderson	303	1936	Tony Manero	282
1905	Willie Anderson	314	1937	Ralph Guldahl	281
1906	Alex Smith	295	1938	Ralph Guldahl	284
1907	Alex Ross	302	1939	Byron Nelson	284-68-70
1908	Fred McLeod	322-77	1940	Lawson Little	287-70
1909	George Sargent	290	1941	Craig Wood	284
1910	Alex Smith	298-71	1942	Ben Hogan	271
1911	John McDermott	307-80	1943–45	No championship: WWII	
1912	John McDermott	294	1946	Lloyd Mangrum	284-72-72
1913	Francis Ouimet	304-72	1947	Lew Worsham	282-69
1914	Walter Hagen	290	1948	Ben Hogan	276
1915	Jerry Travers	297	1949	Cary Middlecoff	286
1916	Chick Evans	286	1950	Ben Hogan	287-69
1917	Jock Hutchinson	292	1951	Ben Hogan	287
1918	No championship: WWI		1952	Julius Boros	281
1919	Walter Hagen	301-77	1953	Ben Hogan	283
1920	Ted Ray	295	1954	Ed Furgol	284
1921	Jim Barnes	289	1955	Jack Fleck	287-69
1922	Gene Sarazen	288	1956	Cary Middlecoff	281
1923	Bobby Jones	296-76	1957	Dick Mayer	282-72
1924	Cyril Walker	297	1958	Tommy Bolt	283
1925	Willie Macfarlane	291-75-72	1959	Billy Casper	282
1926	Bobby Jones	293	1960	Arnold Palmer	280

1961	Gene Littler	281	1978	Andy North	285
1962	Jack Nicklaus	283-71	1979	Hale Irwin	284
1963	Julius Boros	293-71	1980	Jack Nicklaus	272
1964	Ken Venturi	278	1981	David Graham	273
1965	Gary Player	282-71	1982	Tom Watson	282
1966	Billy Casper	278-69	1983	Larry Nelson	280
1967	Jack Nicklaus	275	1984	Fuzzy Zoeller	276-67
1968	Lee Trevino	275	1985	Andy North	279
1969	Orville Moody	281	1986	Raymond Floyd	279
1970	Tony Jacklin	281	1987	Scott Simpson	277
1971	Lee Trevino	280-68	1988	Curtis Strange	278-71
1972	Jack Nicklaus	290	1989	Curtis Strange	278
1973	Johnny Miller	279	1990	Hale Irwin	280-74-3
1974	Hale Irwin	287	1991	Payne Stewart	280-75
1975	Lou Graham	287-71	1992	Tom Kite	285
1976	Jerry Pate	277	1993	Lee Janzen	272
1977	Hubert Green	278	1994	Ernie Els	279-74-4-4

A CHRONOLOGY OF SCORING RECORDS

Over Eighteen Holes:

82—Horace Rawlins, Newport Golf Club, 1895

74—James Foulis, Shinnecock Hills Golf Club, 1896

73—Gil Nicolls, Garden City Golf Club, 1902

73—Willie Anderson, Glen View Club, 1904

68—David Hunter, Englewood Golf Club, 1909

67—Willie Macfarlane, Worcester Country Club, 1925

66—Gene Sarazen, Fresh Meadow Country Club, 1932

65—Jimmy McHale, St. Louis Country Club, 1947

64—Lee Mackey, Merion Golf Club, 1950

63—Johnny Miller, Oakmont Country Club, 1973

Over Seventy-Two Holes:

328—Fred Herd, Myopia Hunt Club, 1898

315—Willie Smith, Baltimore Country Club, 1899

313—Harry Vardon, Chicago Golf Club, 1900

307—Laurie Auchterlonie, Garden City Golf Club, 1902

303—Willie Anderson, Glen View Club, 1904

295—Alex Smith, Onwentsia Club, 1906

290—George Sargent, Englewood Golf Club, 1909

286—Chick Evans, Minikahda Club, 1916

282—Tony Manero, Baltusrol Golf Club, 1936

281—Ralph Guldahl, Oakland Hills Country Club, 1937

276—Ben Hogan, Riviera Country Club, 1948

275—Jack Nicklaus, Baltusrol Golf Club, 1967

272—Jack Nicklaus, Baltusrol Golf Club, 1980

272—Lee Janzen, Baltusrol Golf Club, 1993